THE DAISIES OF AFRICA

Steven Oliver

malcolm down
PUBLISHING

It is not difficult to recommend this remarkable book. A superb example of obedience, humility, honesty, vulnerability, and courageous faith, giving God space to demonstrate His power, faithfulness, and ability to lead and guide. I urge you to read it and be stimulated by Steve and Heather's wonderful story.

Terry Virgo
Founder of Newfrontiers

A remarkable story of prophetic direction from the Lord, a family's obedience despite not easy circumstances, compassion to the poor, and a multi-cultural church planted where there was previously hostility. I enthusiastically commend *The Daisies of Africa* and encourage readers to learn as well as enjoy and to apply the message in their own contexts.

David Devenish
Newfrontiers

The story of *The Daisies of Africa* as depicted in this book is as much about a man of faith – that is Steve – and his family pursuing the purposes of God, as it's about a people. It's a multi-layered story. As you peel one layer, there is Steve and Heather. As you peel another layer you encounter a community called Dihlabeng Church in the small village of Clarens – from humble beginnings to changing the world. Another layer and you get the birth of a worldwide movement of churches represented by faithful men and women spread over six continents. Isn't that how the Bible is designed? From one man called Abraham you get a family, and from that family you get the multitude – read this story of faith and be convinced!

Fusi Mokoena
Leader of the Regions Beyond family of churches

Whoever reads this book and is unmoved by the stories of His grace, His mercy, His power, and His faithfulness, needs to take their pulse to check and see if they've still got life in their bones!

Jeff Kidwell
Pastor, church planter

Copyright © Steven Oliver 2025

First published 2025 by Malcolm Down Publishing Ltd
www.malcolmdown.co.uk

29 28 27 26 25   7 6 5 4 3 2 1

The right of Steven Oliver to be identified as the author of this work has been asserted by him in accordance with the Copyright, Designs and Patents Act 1988.

All rights reserved. No part of this publication may be reproduced, stored in a retrieval system, or transmitted in any other form or by any means, electronic, mechanical, photocopying, recording or otherwise, without the prior permission of the publisher.

British Library Cataloguing in Publication Data
A catalogue record for this book is available from the British Library.

ISBN 978-1-917455-41-1

Scripture quotations marked "NIV" are taken from the Holy Bible, New International Version (Anglicised edition). Copyright © 1979, 1984, 2011 Biblica. Used by permission of Hodder & Stoughton Ltd, an Hachette UK company. All rights reserved. "NIV" is a registered trademark of Biblica. UK trademark number 1448790.

Scripture quotations marked "NASB" are taken from the
Holy Bible, NEW AMERICAN STANDARD BIBLE®,
Copyright © 1960,1962,1963,1968,1971,1972,1973,1975,1977, 1995 by The Lockman Foundation. Used by permission.

Scripture quotations marked "NKJV" are taken from the Holy Bible, New King James Version®. Copyright © 1982 by Thomas Nelson. Used by permission. All rights reserved.

Scripture quotations marked "ESV" are taken from the Holy Bible, English Standard Version (Anglicised). Published by HarperCollins Publishers © 2001 Crossway Bibles, a publishing ministry of Good News Publishers. Used by permission. All rights reserved.

Scripture quotations marked "AMP" are taken from the Amplified Bible Copyright © 2015 by The Lockman Foundation, La Habra, CA 90631, USA. All rights reserved.

Cover design by Esther Kotecha
Art direction by Sarah Grace

Printed in the UK

FOR HEATHER

Thank you for saying "yes" all those years ago on
Hout Bay beach in Cape Town, South Africa,
on that wonderful sunny afternoon.

We had no idea what lay ahead—
but what an adventure it's been!

Thank you for your faithfulness through it all.

CONTENTS

Acknowledgements	9
Foreword	11
1. In The Beginning	13
2. Angus Houston – Sent by Christ!	23
3. Step By Step	33
4. A New Message	41
5. Break Camp and Advance	47
6. Encounter	57
7. A Change Of Heart	67
8. Man of Peace	73
9. The People Are Waiting	83
10. It Is Time!	95
11. Heading North to Clarens	111
12. Finding a Name – Dihlabeng	121
13. Preparing to Plant	129
14. The Birth – Dihlabeng Church	135
15. My Name Is Justice, I've Come To Be Saved!	143
16. Rural Revival	149
17. I Will Build My Church	155

18.	Who Will You Become?	167
19.	Standing on Others' Shoulders	177
20.	Forceful Advance	185
21.	Do You Not Know Who You Are?	199
22.	A New Course	209
23.	Promised Land	215
24.	Growing Fruitfulness and Coming of Age	227
25.	Sons in the Household	235
26.	It Was Raw, But Effective	243
27.	Remembering the Poor	249
28.	I'll Go!	255
29.	I Can Do That!	263
30.	We Tore Ourselves Away	267
31.	On To The Regions Beyond	273

ACKNOWLEDGEMENTS

It has been a tremendous privilege to write this, the first of two books, detailing the early part of our journey prior to the birth of the Regions Beyond family of churches. With each page, I was constantly reminded that this is much more than *my* story.

I'm enormously grateful to my wife, Heather, and my three sons, Cameron, Richard, and Adam, who sacrificed so much over many years to allow this story to be written. No words can adequately capture the joys and the pain of all we embraced together. You are my true heroes of the faith. Thank you.

I have also tried my best to introduce many friends who have played a part in our lives, and in the growth of our churches and the movement of churches we've been a part of. Sadly, there are many more who I could have mentioned, but I hope they too will celebrate what God has done. Thank you to each one of you. I hope you will share my joy as you read this account of *The Daisies of Africa*.

A special thank you to Navaz D'Cruz, who journeyed with me daily as I wrote this book. Your guidance, insights, and continual encouragement kept me focused and on track. Thank you for every hour spent working through the chapters – your keen eye for necessary changes was invaluable. I hope our partnership in this task will bless many.

And to Heather, thank you again, for faithfully reading and re-reading chapter after chapter. I couldn't have done this without you.

Lastly, to my Dihlabeng Church family – this is your story. From humble beginnings, we were privileged to see God do wonderful things. May it long continue. All the proceeds of this book will go to you – toward your call to continue in His grace, and into many fruitful years ahead.

Steve Oliver

Contact Regions Beyond
www.regionsbeyond.net
Info@regionsbeyond.net

FOREWORD

Driving home from Scotland, a five-hundred-mile journey, my wife Sue read aloud Steve's book, *The Daisies of Africa*. Throughout the journey we laughed, we cried, and reminisced, and often said, "I never knew that!" It brought back memories of the last thirty years of friendship with Steve and Heather Oliver.

In 1996 I was invited to be the guest speaker at two leadership conferences in South Africa and I heard the strange story of the "Daisies of Africa" man, and was surprised when, in the middle of the night, I felt God speak to me that I was to seek him out. No one seemed to know who he was, they just knew his story. But we were introduced to Jeff and Viv Kidwell who told us his name was Steve Oliver and we would be meeting him in Durban. I did meet Steve and I think we both felt an instant bonding. Sue and I spent three days with him and Heather at their beautiful farm. I remember the second morning, Steve shared with me his encounter with God in Toronto and the prophetic call he received to go to the daisies of Africa. He also shared that God had said to him that, from humble beginnings, the nations of the world would be reached with the gospel of Jesus. To his surprise I said, "That's wonderful!" Apparently, I was the first person to think he was not totally mad!

I told him that I had also left my professional career to take on a small struggling Baptist church, how the church had grown and was spiritually renewed on a New Testament foundation, and was now involved with several other nations.

At theological college, where I majored in church history, I remembered other pioneers, the Moravians, William Carey, Hudson Taylor, C.T. Studd, Gladys Aylward, Jim and Elizabeth Elliott, and many others who had a similar encounter and persevered, despite much opposition. All the setbacks, disappointments, and failures you will read about in this book speak for themselves, that what God promised Steve and Heather is now on the ground and reaching many nations.

Sue and I loved reading this book. It's very honest and informative and I trust that you, like us, will not just enjoy it but will be stirred, perhaps even convicted, and also convinced of the greater works that have yet to be done, which Jesus spoke of in John 14:12, which I believe is about taking the gospel to the ends of the earth.

Ray Lowe
International minister, pastor and church planter

Chapter 1
IN THE BEGINNING

My heart pounded with anticipation as I joined many others and made my way to the front of Meadowridge Baptist Church in Cape Town, South Africa. Reverend Roger Voke had just delivered an impassioned gospel message to those of us attending the evening service – his vibrancy, passion, and energy made clear why Jesus Christ had died for humanity, and I felt I could not ignore it. The truth of his words moved me deeply, and he spoke with such urgency that evening, emphasising his point by pounding his hand hard on the frame of the raised pulpit. Nobody moved an inch. I vividly remember the way he raised his voice to make a point; fully attentive, we sat and listened to every word. Now, in response to the invitation, we made the journey down from the upstairs balcony, where we teenagers gathered for the evening service. The usher led us to a place to stand as the whole congregation sang that well-known old hymn.

> *Just as I am, without one plea,*
> *But that Thy blood was shed for me,*
> *And that Thou bid'st me come to Thee,*
> *Oh, Lamb of God I come! I come!*[1]

I was fourteen years old.

---

1. 'Just As I Am' by Charlotte Elliott (1835). Public Domain.

Young once

About ten of us stood at the front that evening, and I noticed a lovely young friend, Heather Carney, standing to my right, who responded in the same way I did. At the time, I had no idea we had just begun what would become a lifelong journey of togetherness in Christ. We were encouraged to repeat the prayer spoken for us and, with all sincerity, surrender our lives to Jesus Christ. It was a remarkable, life-changing evening in many ways.

They say Cape Town, South Africa, is one of the best cities in the world to live in, and with all its natural beauty, it certainly has much to offer. The large peninsula juts out into the Indian and Atlantic oceans, offering spectacular views and weather systems that originate from the southern oceans, earning it the nickname Cape of Storms. My earliest memories of growing up in the suburb of Meadowridge, some twenty kilometres from the city centre, are of a wonderful childhood. I was born into a loving family, the youngest of four children, and life was as settled as anyone could wish for. My father, Richard, was a hard-working man in the garment industry, and my mother, Maureen, was an attentive stay-at-home mother. As a family on the rise economically, we enjoyed the mountains and the beaches, with a special highlight being my father's passion for beach fishing. We used long rods to cast way out beyond the breakers, and I have many memories of him drawing large Steenbras and Kabeljou (fish found in these waters) to the shoreline. On one occasion, I remember the Kabeljou being taller than me as my father battled to lift it upright. Across the road from our post-World War II home was the Meadowridge forest, composed mainly of tall pine trees. As a young child, the forest always seemed enormous and filled with memories of great adventures among the trees in this quiet suburb.

Life seemed much simpler then for me, a young teenager, but I'm sure it was different for my parents as they made their way in life with a young family. They had always ensured that we attended Sunday school from a very young age, but they only joined us at the local Presbyterian church on special occasions, namely Christmas and Easter. It was only much later that I learned that they had once been fully devoted to a local Christian cult community, only to leave on bad terms due to the heavy-handedness of the leaders, leadership failures and the extreme burden of legalism practised by the church. The story I was told was that my mother, Maureen, had told my father, "Either we leave these people, or I am leaving you!" My father, Richard, obliged, not wanting to lose my mother and ties were cut with this overbearing cult. Now, looking back with understanding, I can see how painful this process must have been for them. Such was the nature of the negative experience they had had in their church life that my mother was not too pleased to hear of my decision on that life-changing Sunday night at Meadowridge Baptist Church. She was happy for me to fully participate in the active youth group, but now, according to her, I was getting too serious. Being the youngest in the family, I had always had a very special relationship with her, and this was one of the few times I ever saw her truly displeased with me. What made it even worse was when I placed a large modern graphic of a Jesus image on the wall above my bed, and suffice it to say we had "words" about this on several occasions! However, my commitment was very real to me, and I continued to grow in my faith.

The youth club

I smile when I remember my introduction to the church. Life for me at the time meant playing lots of sports: rugby for my school in the mornings and soccer for a local club in the afternoons, and when I was not on the field, I was spearfishing at the coast, some twenty-five kilometres away. My introduction to this church community came when my soccer captain, another energetic young man, told me that he had heard about the number of amazing young teenage girls who were attending the youth club at the local Baptist church. So, we decided to go check it out. We were amazed at the vibrancy of this youth gathering, and whoever had reported that several attractive young ladies were attending was certainly not wrong; we were thrilled. However, the atmosphere of togetherness and their evident love of God soon had my fullest attention. What I was witnessing was not the stale religion that I was accustomed to. There was evidence of vibrant life among these young people. They redefined fun in every sense of the word.

Although my home environment and life were filled with sporting activities and school, I felt I had "come home" and loved my church community, so much so that I even started considering Bible college. However, my mother's response to that thought was not very encouraging. I found it hard to miss the most casual prayer meeting and loved the encouragement I received from those who had walked this journey for many years. A newly married couple, Brian and Marion Devlin, had been given the role of leading the youth, and they profoundly influenced our lives with the outstanding commitment they displayed. I loved and admired them. They opened their home for me to drop in at any time.

Our community of teenagers and young adults continued to grow, and those were delightful days. All this happened at the height of the Jesus Revolution, which took place among the hippies in California, USA. This movement spread globally and ushered in a much less formal understanding of the church. Many hours were spent listening to the gospel band Love Song and the beautiful melodies they produced. Throughout these days, I enjoyed a growing friendship with Heather Carney. We were baptised on the same morning, attended discipleship classes together, and fully participated in the vibrant youth work at our local church. Heather had grown up one road away from the church facility and, like me, had made her journey to knowing God, as her parents showed little interest. Sport and school kept me busy, but I loved the growing youth community in those days.

Young love

In April 1977, my brother Alan was to be married, and my parents encouraged me to bring a partner to this special event. Fighting all my fears and subsequent nervousness, I took the big step and invited Heather to accompany me, and, to my delight, she agreed to come. I still remember the day I went to collect her for the afternoon wedding and met her father, Mike, at the door. At six-foot-seven-inches tall, he towered over me! I was thrilled to learn that he was a gentle giant, and over the years he became a very close friend, more than he was to be my father-in-law five years later. Heather was everything I had dreamed she would be, and we had the most wonderful evening. I was smitten!

It wasn't long before Heather and I realised that we were meant for each other, and we became inseparable. We shared a common interest in our love for the mountains and beaches of Cape Town, and we had a great circle of friends in common. Heather had a genuine fondness for animals, and we would "steal" a neighbour's dog for walks on the beach, only to return him hours later, sodden and dirty. It must have been quite a mystery for the owners trying to understand how Bruce got so wet and salty! Life was full of fun and adventure in those early days. We were both in our final year of school, and our growing relationship didn't help our school marks, much to our parents' dismay.

Conscription and separation

Sadly, our togetherness was not to be for long as a two-year army conscription awaited all young men of European descent (white South Africans). The Apartheid system of "Separate Development" in South Africa had become one of severe oppression of the indigenous African people-groups, and tensions had risen to a boiling point in our nation, where both the police force and the army were mobilised to keep control. It was a thankless task. Furthermore, international isolation and a fear of communism stoked the fires of nationalism among the white population. As an eighteen-year-old, I found myself on the frontline of a bush war on the northern border of South West Africa (now Namibia) and southern Angola. Our days and nights in the remote sections of the Caprivi Strip were spent on patrol, and I think it was there that the beautiful African landscape stole my heart. It was there that I discovered my pioneering spirit, as I always volunteered to "walk point", which meant being way ahead of the main body of soldiers, acting as the "eyes and ears" of the platoon. Many years later, when we moved to Dubai, I was asked by an Angolan member of our church if I had ever been to his country. Sadly, I had to reply, "Yes! But I was armed and uninvited!" We both laughed and hugged at that crazy thought and promised to arrange a much friendlier visit!

Heather had finished school at the same time as I had, and she had begun her first job, which led to her becoming a legal secretary in the city. We maintained our relationship by writing copious letters that crisscrossed Southern Africa regularly. It was hard to maintain constant contact, and even harder to keep our walk with God alive, which we sadly neglected. Life was very confusing in those days, with our separation, the political climate, and uncertainty about the future in South Africa.

Push-ups for letters!

Army life was harsh. It was the indoctrination into an ungodly philosophy that left one feeling very confused by the mixture of religion and ideology that led to Christian nationalism in its worst form. It held the view that God liked some people groups but hated others. Unfortunately, we were supposedly among the former; what a lie. Slowly, my lack of interest in God, as well as many poor choices, robbed me of any relationship I had had with the loving heavenly Father I had met four years previously.

During this time, while we were fighting a bush war in southern Angola, all letters from Heather dried up. It was excruciatingly painful, as I was madly in love with her and believed we would marry as soon as I got discharged from the army. One month passed, not a single letter. A second month was almost through when one morning on parade, I heard the duty sergeant shout, "Oliver!" You did not take your own sweet time to respond when the sergeant bellows your name with such urgency! I arrived before him, displaying the finest respect, only to be lambasted for receiving twelve perfume-soaked lilac-coloured letters! "If you want them, it will cost you twenty push-ups per letter!" was the instruction given to me. No decision was needed there! I lost no time hitting the floor, and I remember sweating and pumping my arms with every bit of energy I had as I wanted those letters so badly. I was a fit and strong young man in those days and well-equipped to pay the price for my treasured letters, and I was overjoyed to have letters from my beloved once again. I also made many friends that day, as the letters filled our shared tent with the most wonderful scent that reminded us of all our homes and loved ones far away. I then discovered that her letters were sent to another part of the South West African bush. When they finally found out where I was, they faithfully sent them to my company based in Etale in the Caprivi Strip, Namibia, even despite an overdose of "Youth Dew" perfume on each letter. Heather's love was confirmed, and mine was rekindled. How grateful I was to be able to live again.

The conflict in the border area intensified, and I lost some good friends in those days. It was a pointless and unjust campaign, like so many are. Upon demobilisation at the end of my two-year duty, I returned to Cape Town, and Heather and I began to seek employment.

Back home

I was never very clear on a career path and held quite a sober view of myself. Sadly, I had no interest in studying, but I enjoyed building a life with Heather and, overall, I was somewhat disillusioned with life after my military service. We decided not to get married but instead move in together, a trend that had become common among people my age. Our small, rented apartment became a lovely home, overlooking Table Mountain, Cape Town's jewel. Those were happy yet confusing times as we navigated what we had once known and now embraced a very different set of values. By then, the church was a distant memory, and we had adopted different self-centred values. However, it didn't take long for Heather and me to realise that we wanted to get married, and in December 1982, we celebrated a wonderful wedding day. We returned to a beautiful stone Anglican church in Constantia for the ceremony, very close to where we had grown up. It was a splendid day.

Already, there was a "nations bug" in us, and we used every single South African Rand that we had to travel around Europe for an entire month, and we loved it. No sooner had we settled back into our life in Cape Town than I was approached by a boyhood friend to ask if I would consider starting a business with him. After many hours of discussion and lots of planning, Astron Systems (Pty) Ltd was born six months later.

Chapter 2

ANGUS HOUSTON – SENT BY CHRIST!

Astron Systems (Pty) Ltd was a complicated business. Heather and I, along with our friends, launched the business in 1984, believing that we had all the skills and passion to succeed, despite the fact that only five out of every hundred new businesses survive more than five years in our nation. I resigned from my secure employment with a large multinational manufacturing company and we began the journey of establishing our business. With our hearts full of dreams and enthusiasm and having settled our product lines, we set about finding a suitable name for the company. We were disappointed by the number of times the Companies Registrar in Pretoria rejected our chosen name. One afternoon, Heather said, "How about Astron?" She explained, "An Astron is the brightest star in a galaxy?" There was immediate approval, and a few days later we were thrilled to receive confirmation that our new company's name had been accepted and it was registered in 1984. Thus began a great adventure at the age of twenty-four.

Our passion and self-belief far outweighed our working capital, and life was a constant struggle to find resources to fund an ever-growing business. My partner and designer was an incredibly gifted man who could turn ground-breaking ideas into products. With innovative marketing, we quickly gained a growing influence in the electronic security business sector. Little did people know we were "running on the smell of an oil rag"! However, the company continued to grow and grow.

As our market share continued to grow, we were taken aback when approached by others in the industry interested in stocking and selling our products. I remember long nights when we even taught Heather to solder circuit boards, and everyone carried part of the load in our production unit. We found a beautiful office in the heart of the city, in Radio House, Loop Street, Cape Town, and our staff complement multiplied, as did our production efficiency. Our success soon led us to establish franchises nationwide, enabling the company to grow based on our innovative product range. My primary role was to establish the new franchises, and I began to travel the breadth of our nation as opportunities arose. Looking back, I can see how influential that period was in preparing me for what I would ultimately be doing in the church through church planting. It was satisfying work for me, but there was both success and failure in opening these new franchises.

Our success in these challenging and exciting times led us to an increasingly hedonistic lifestyle. We indulged in all the material pleasures life had to offer, but were, by now, far away from God and not in the slightest bit interested in church. We built our company ethos around the mantra of "becoming millionaires by the age of thirty and never leaving Cape Town"! We were extremely proud of our achievements, and I cringe when I consider how self-centred and arrogant we had become.

Enter Angus

With our growing influence, we thought it would be beneficial to add a sales manager position to our management team. We placed an advertisement in the Cape Town press, providing complete details of the high standards we had set. So, we began interviewing potential candidates. One afternoon, Heather, who was now working full-time in our front office, knocked on my door to announce the arrival of our next applicant. As she stepped aside, a man named Angus Houston marched in. His wide, purposeful gait spoke much of who he was. He was smartly dressed in a suit and tie, looking very professional with his large, square briefcase, which he confidently placed on my desk before extending his hand to introduce himself. Heather politely offered him a cup of tea, which he accepted with enthusiasm. I immediately sensed that standing before me was a man with a big personality. I liked him. As Heather fetched the tea, Angus proceeded to open his briefcase with great gusto as if wanting to hold centre stage. I expected him to retrieve his CV, but to my shock, he took a well-worn New American Standard Bible and his CV out of his briefcase. At this moment, Heather came back in with the tea tray. Noticing the Bible on the desk in front of Angus, she shot me a wide-eyed expression across the room before making a hasty exit. My life was about to change.

Mr Houston took over the interview. "Before I speak to you about my wish to work for your company, which I am very impressed with, I want to share something about myself. I want you to know that I am a Spirit-filled Christian. Sundays, I give entirely to my church. Wednesday evenings are reserved for my house group, and the rest of my week, I will dedicate to your company. I would love to work for you." That was it.

I cannot remember how I regained my composure after that introduction, but as the rest of the interview progressed, I was quite struck by the life that emanated from his eyes and the joy that seemed to flow from his heart. I had never met anyone quite like this. He was so secure in who he was, so enthusiastic and courageous. It was not long before I invited him to join our company, which caused a bit of consternation in the office. Heather still laughs about it! Angus and his wife-to-be, Hildur, became our lifelong friends.

Angus's father had the wonderful role of being the farm manager for one of Stellenbosch's top wine farms, and the family had a home on the estate. Stellenbosch is renowned worldwide for producing the finest wines. Coastal breezes, good soil and adequate sunshine are all found in Stellenbosch, making for the finest cultivars. On weekends, we made the hour-long journey to Stellenbosch and enjoyed the outstanding beauty of the prestigious Rustenburg wine estate. They were fun-filled days, and both Heather and I have very fond memories of getting to know and becoming a part of Angus's wider family. Over the following weeks and months, Angus's impact on our company grew, and great blessings seemed to follow his every action. Our sales grew, the atmosphere in the business seemed to blossom with life, and we became very good friends. He joined in with all our fun but was a man true to his word in that we never saw him on Wednesday evenings or Sundays. When we faced real struggles as a company, Angus would volunteer to pray for us, and his prayers seemed well honoured. Each week, without fail, we would receive an invitation to visit Stellenbosch Christian Fellowship, his local church community. I became highly skilled at finding excuses and evading his every request for almost a year. We were determined to keep our distance from the church, even though we could see the impact it had on his life. Whichever church he belonged to could be extremely proud of this passionate and enthusiastic member, Angus Houston.

Tragedy!

A year after employing Angus Houston, I received a telephone call late one afternoon that was to change our lives forever. My brother Alan called to tell me that my fifty-five-year-old mother, Maureen, had been diagnosed with a severe form of Lymphoma cancer. Listening to the details made it feel like ice-cold water ran through my veins. I tried to ask appropriate questions, and take in and process this tragic news. Cancer treatment in 1986 was not as advanced as it is today, but my brother assured me that the doctors would do all they could. So began a two-year journey, which eventually ended with her passing away late in 1987. It is remarkable how God always places the right people around you when you face life's tragedies.

What grace! No sooner did Angus learn of our sad news than he mobilised his church to pray; he arranged for his pastor to visit my ailing mother and provided all the care we could ever wish for. Over this time, I realised that his church community was nothing like the more formal type of church I'd experienced as a teenager. It also became apparent to me that my life was completely bankrupt, even though I had made a commitment to Jesus Christ in my early teens. Having hardened my heart, I had nothing to lean on except Heather and friends. Heather was a constant pillar of support for me in those days, as she was very close to my parents and could step in at just the right times. When we visited my parents, I had no words of comfort for my mother in her ailing state, only inner turmoil and anger that arose in those desperate days. I had set a course in my life to do it my way, and now I was truly the most isolated man anyone could be. Such was the low state of my emotions that, at times, I chose not even to visit my father and mother, even though I was so close to them. This desperate battle, with all its ups and downs, finally ended two years later when my mother, Maureen, passed away. We were numbed by the news, filled with guilt and unanswered questions. It was only later that Heather and I came to learn that she had made a fresh commitment to Christ two weeks before her death when my sister-in-law, Merle, led her back to Christ. Even with this comforting news, we were captive to our anger and unanswered questions about why such a fruitful life would come to such a tragic end. We tried our best to move on and comfort my struggling father, but life seemed incredibly empty.

The turning point

It was soon after my mother's death that Heather and I finally accepted Angus's invitation to visit Stellenbosch Christian Fellowship. Maybe we had softened, or perhaps

What a welcome we received that afternoon! Heather and I hugged and celebrated. We had come home.

Later that day, I called our dear friend Angus and told him everything that had happened. He was overjoyed and told me that the whole church would be thrilled to hear the news, as they had all been praying for us. We received so many calls and messages from our new family in Stellenbosch. We did not know all this had been taking place and that so many had been praying on our behalf.

Thank you, my friend

So often, we think the "full-time" church leaders are responsible for "building the church". Angus had a different understanding, for which I am so grateful. In his employment, Angus Houston was a true ambassador of Jesus Christ, and he fulfilled his calling so well. The nations rejoice because of people like Angus, and we celebrate them. Whenever I see a new church planted or individuals turning to Christ, I always try to remember to message Angus and his wonderful wife, Hildur – "All because of your faithfulness, my friend!" Thank you.

Chapter 3

STEP BY STEP

Our response to God's wonderful grace that afternoon, as we knelt on our living room floor, ushered in an entirely new and somewhat challenging period in our lives. Many adjustments were needed to our lives if we were to be true to the contrite prayers we had prayed. All the events of the past few weeks started to have a significant impact on our lives as we adjusted to the change of heart. Each weekend, we would travel out to Stellenbosch to join the church community that met in the Van Der Stel Gymnasium. Angus played a key role in including us in as many activities as possible, and it was comforting to see the level of care provided by the church leadership. We were so grateful for what God had done in us that we took advantage of every opportunity for fellowship, making many new friends in the process. Stellenbosch is such a beautiful country town; initially, we didn't find the constant travel very difficult. With its Cape Dutch, white-walled buildings and fantastic restaurants, Stellenbosch became a big part of our lives, and with our growing friendship with Angus and Hildur, our weekends became very full and satisfying.

Home building

However, various other situations began to shape our future. Heather and I had purchased our first home in the northern suburbs of Cape Town, in a suburb called Edgemead. We were very proud of our beautiful little house and worked hard to make it a base from which we could build a family. With Heather's exceptional decorating skills and ability to provide a comfortable home, it was a wonderful place to live and entertain our friends. Before marrying Hildur, Angus would stay over on many occasions rather than return to Stellenbosch, so life was fun and full. Even as we settled into the new rhythms of life, we became unsettled with where we lived, mainly because we had always lived on the opposite, far end of the Cape Peninsula. And so, we dreamed of moving back to the area we felt was truly home. Practically speaking, this seemed an impossibility due to the high cost of homes in the southern suburbs of Cape Town.

However, one Saturday afternoon, Heather and I drove into one of the most prestigious areas of Cape Town's southern suburbs, called Constantia. With its proximity to the mountains and incredible heritage and beauty, it was truly the ideal area to live in, but one that was only a dream for us. Turning a corner in this leafy suburb, we saw a small A4 board advertising "Plots for sale" tied to a fence post. As we entered the signposted Zomerlust Avenue, we were overwhelmed by the magnificence of this piece of land up for sale, as it bordered a greenbelt area with lush vegetation, a stream, and breath-taking views of the Constantiaberg Mountains. On enquiry, we discovered, to our surprise, that it would be affordable if we could manage a small deposit. To our absolute amazement, we found ourselves the owners of one of the plots of land in this idyllic location. With this unexpected opportunity, life took a sudden turn, and we knew a significant move was imminent.

Bends and turns in the road

The second aspect that began to influence and shape our future was my growing unsettledness in our company. My renewed faith, along with an increasing love for the church and the enjoyment of the Stellenbosch-based community, began to adjust my values and life priorities. This change in me led to growing tensions in the business partnership we had enjoyed for so long. The company was now six years old and required increasing investment in both time and finances. We invested in the latest production machinery, and our designs and products continued to advance. However, our growing influence had an adverse impact on our financial stability. In hindsight, I can recognise how my worldview was changing, but at the time, this was not something I was able to recognise or acknowledge. Instead, I foolishly thought that my business partner was being inflexible, and it was his attitude that was causing all the unnecessary tension.

Amid this ever-changing landscape of our lives, Heather and I began designing our ideal home for the newly acquired plot of land, never realising that God had very different plans for us. As we were new to the building process and the associated costs, we found that we had to repeatedly reduce the size of the home until the design became something we could afford. The house was unrecognisable from our first concept to the outcome, and we were somewhat deflated in the process. Six months in, there was now feverish activity in Zomerlust Avenue as our soon-to-be neighbours began to build on their land. During this time of great uncertainty, we received an unexpected phone call asking if we would consider selling our land, as it was the only one that had not yet shown signs of development. Unbeknown to us, the value of the land had doubled over the six months we had owned it, and we quickly settled in our hearts that we should sell it and buy something more in line with our budget. Our neighbours were building "palaces", and it felt wrong to be considering a small cottage. So, it wasn't long before we had sold our land and found a beautiful small cottage not far from where we would have built. We loved it and immediately set about making it home.

Where we lived led to another real challenge for Heather and me, as we were now living very far from our church community in Stellenbosch, and attending regularly became a challenge. The leadership was very understanding and helpful, advising us to move to a community closer to hand where we could play a more meaningful role in the church's life. They advised us to consider a growing community called The Vineyard. It was an independent church with no ties to any denomination or church network and came highly recommended by our present leaders in Stellenbosch. The Vineyard community met on Sunday evenings in a commercial area near us, and Heather and I made our way there at the first possible opportunity. At the time, we were unaware that they had five congregations that met around the peninsula each Sunday morning.

To our delight, we found an atmosphere of real grace, friendship and purpose, and we also recognised that this church had a pronounced leaning towards multi-cultural togetherness, something that was still very new in our divided nation. At this point, freedom and equality in South Africa, under Nelson Mandela's leadership, was still six years away. Still, it was refreshing to see the intentionality of this community to fully represent the nation in which we lived and we celebrated it. No sooner had we found a place to sit than the meeting started. Talented musicians led us in wonderful worship, and we began to feel settled. The Vineyard was everything we were told it would be. Leading the evening service that day was a larger-than-life personality who looked vaguely familiar. Those of us who were first-time visitors were asked to raise our hands so we could be formally welcomed. It was then that this leader, Jeff Kidwell, said, "It's wonderful to welcome Steve and Heather Oliver here tonight! I met Steve two years ago in a business context and welcome both of you!" which caught both Heather and me off guard. To my surprise, I discovered that Jeff Kidwell, who had previously worked at a large insurance company with which I had had business dealings, was now a full-time pastor at The Vineyard. Jeff's incredible ability to remember people and their names had such an impact on us, and his warmth quickly won our hearts. His ability to lovingly connect with us made our transition to The Vineyard so easy. He introduced us to his wife, Viv, and a deep friendship and bond developed between us. They were more than friends; they were spiritual parents, family, and such inspiring role models for Heather and me, as we were finding our way in faith. They had four children, and we loved being with them whenever possible. And even more quickly, their love for God and His church began to rub off on us. Jeff and Viv lived just five minutes from our new home, and we quickly joined The Vineyard Plumstead congregation, which Jeff also led on Sunday mornings. How grateful we were to have leaders who were like "fathers and mothers" in the church.

Happy, but an empty nest

Before moving into our new home and church, Heather and I had a growing desire to start a family. We had celebrated six years of marriage, the business was established, albeit through a great struggle, and it just felt like that season had arrived for us to have a family. Sadly, falling pregnant proved to be a real difficulty for us, and a few months turned into two years. For anyone who has experienced the loneliness of the struggle to conceive, it was pretty desperate at times. We sought medical help, which took us on a challenging journey. One evening, the topic arose, and we shared our struggles with Jeff and Viv. In his inimitable way, Jeff announced they would come over and pray for us the following evening. As planned, Jeff and Viv arrived and quickly directed us into our bedroom. There we were before God, and Heather and I shared a burden we had carried for so many years, which was the guilt of having lived together for two years before our marriage. With Jeff and Viv's kind help, we released this to God and felt the weight of guilt dissipate as forgiveness flooded in. Jeff and Viv then laid hands on us to receive healing and conceive. It was a truly special and intimate moment. Jeff closed by saying, "Remember, faith without works is dead! Now, let's have a glass of wine!" That's the Jeff we had come to love! With much laughter, we retired to the living room.

Good news!

Close to our company offices in Loop Street, Cape Town, was a small Lutheran church building built in the early stages of the development of the Mother City. Having received these deeply felt prayers, I felt led to fast for Heather and me, and each lunchtime, Angus also joined me. We would go to this quaint little building and seek God together. Those were special times, and a few months later, I received the most wonderful phone call from Heather to say, "It's confirmed, we're going to have a baby!" I was enormously grateful to God and equally proud of Heather, who blossomed during her pregnancy. Nine months later, we were blessed with Cameron, the first of our three boys.

Jeff and Viv's constant care and encouragement meant that we were growing healthily in our walk with God and loved the church. Heather, with her new little baby, was as busy as ever and fully involved with the other mothers in the church. One Sunday, Jeff introduced fourteen new leaders to the church, which, in that moment, unlocked a deep desire in my heart. Watching from the congregation, I felt a deep desire to lead others, even though the thought of it filled me with fear. Despite these personal fears, I began to prepare myself to be diligent with my studies and time with Jeff, getting ready for the possibility that Jeff might one day ask if we would be willing to lead a small group in our home. So began a leadership journey that continues today, and what a privilege it has been to lead others.

Chapter 4

A NEW MESSAGE

The Vineyard Church then underwent a change in leadership, with a new lead pastor. Under the guidance of Terry Virgo from the Newfrontiers family of churches, we were informed that a young English couple, Simon and Lindsey Pettit, and their family would be emigrating to lead our multi-congregation church. Change is never easy, but there was great excitement as everyone prepared for their coming. Then the day arrived; instead of coming to church in our regular casual clothes, one of the fun-loving older men in our congregation felt it would be fun to shock Simon and Lindsey and all wear collars and ties for their arrival! It worked! As Simon stood before us to bring his first greeting, one could see the confusion on his face with this formal group sitting before him. After making him sweat for a while, there was a great shout, and we quickly stripped the ties off our necks, amidst much laughter and joyous banter. Simon was visibly relieved and so began his engagement with our quirky South African culture and humour. Not only did we receive a new leadership couple, but also a new message.

As Simon began to function in those early days, a journey of transforming us into a true apostolic base (a sending and receiving church base) began. His message was immersed in the grand narrative of God and the part we as believers were called to play. Our heads quickly lifted in anticipation of a growing expectation that we would be involved in something much larger than the local church. Not everyone understood or embraced this new call upon us, but I felt I naturally understood Simon's message. My heart would burn as I heard about the nations and the necessity for cross-cultural ministry as an expression of the church and of the unreached people around the earth. The resonance of the Spirit was strong within my heart, and I began to discover something for which I was willing to give my all. We soon discovered that we had a very special gift among us, which led to an inspiring and exciting church life. It was a great privilege to be part of that transition.

Baptism in the Holy Spirit

Our local congregation in Plumstead thrived under Jeff's leadership. Jeff brought a teaching about "Baptism in the Spirit" one morning. Referencing the prophet Joel's promise and the disciples' experience in Acts 2, he eloquently instilled in us a hunger for what he called being baptised by the Spirit. With the promise of deeper fellowship with God, a release of power and the accompanying gifts of the Spirit, I was ready when the call came to respond. Whatever measure God had for me, I wanted it. Two of our community leaders gathered around me and prayed quietly. I had just heard how tongues of fire and a mighty wind rushed upon Jesus' disciples, so I was full of expectation. No fire, no wind. Yet, a strange, quiet warmth flooded my heart, followed by the first few words of a "spiritual language" as experienced by those at Pentecost. After the prayers, I was both grateful and a little disappointed, as I had hoped for so much more. Had I truly been empowered? That question was answered two weeks later.

A fishy tale

An hour and a half up the coast from Cape Town is the beautiful fishing village of Hermanus. Renowned for its stunning coastal walks and the annual whale migration, Hermanus is a fabulous place to escape and rejuvenate. Heather and I enjoyed many holidays there and were especially fond of this small, beautiful seaside village with a picturesque harbour. Our dear friends Angus and Hildur also had a son, Jared, and we decided to join them and head to Hermanus for a weekend break. Sadly, it was one of the wettest weekends you could ever imagine! It poured incessantly, so we could not leave the house, especially with two small toddlers. After two days inside, Angus and I had severe cabin fever, so we asked the wives if we could explore the town, which we did. Driving through the village, we were amazed at how dreary and quiet everything was, except for a small village pub with a dull light shining inside. We decided to go in and see if they had a snooker table, which indeed they did. Over a rather poor game of snooker, I shared with Angus all that was happening in our church.

What, the devil?

We'd recently enjoyed C.J. Mahaney's ministry, and I related the profound truth he had taught from Job's life experiences. I was obviously very excited and animated about what I was sharing because out of the dark recesses of the bar came a deep, angry voice: "Don't speak about Him [Jesus] here!"

In the far corner of the dark room, we could barely make out the form of a large man. His hair was long and shaggy, only outdone by a bushy beard that almost covered his face. It was hard to make out his features, so Angus and I approached him. I introduced us and said, "We're sorry if our conversation offends you, but it's not possible for us not to speak about Jesus!" My exuberance was a bit of a surprise to me as this type of conversation was certainly a first in my case.

"If you knew who I am, you wouldn't speak about Him here!" was his gruff response. He was a young man, but he was large and imposing in his scruffy state.

"Who are you?" I asked. With what felt like the atmosphere of some awful horror movie, he went on to explain that he was a Satanist who lived with six witches in a coven in the town. Before I could catch the words, I replied, "Well, you can be free of all that!"

"How?" he asked.

"Jesus can set you free!" I told him and continued, "If you want to be free, come to our place, and we'll pray for you, and you'll be free." Angus took a napkin and scribbled down the address of the house where we were staying, and after wishing him well, we headed home, never for a moment thinking he would take us up on our offer. We laughed when we told the wives of our strange encounter in the dingy bar.

Encounter of a real kind

The rain had continued unabated. After it was dark and we had finished our dinner, there was a loud knock on the front door on the lower level. It was a double-storey home, and so Angus and I, now contemplating who that might be, gingerly headed downstairs. I laugh at it now, but as we approached the door, a mighty flash of lightning struck, backlighting the apparition at the door and exposing the outline of a large, drenched, and hairy man. He looked horrific, but we slowly opened the door. "You said I could be set free?" he announced in a small voice.

"Yes, come inside." Our response was not as full of confidence as it was when we were at the downtown bar, but here he was! We led him upstairs, and when Heather and Hildur saw this mighty apparition, they grabbed the boys and made a hasty exit for the downstairs bedrooms.

The living room was large and had an L-shaped lounge suite, Angus sitting at one end and I at the other. Clive, as he had introduced himself, sat next to me. He was contrite and serious about getting his life back together, which made the early stages of our conversation quite easy. I reached over, placed my right hand on his burly shoulder, and asked him if he genuinely wanted to be free. He nodded slowly, and then, with the evilest voice one can ever imagine, came from the demon holding him captive, spoke to us and said, "He is mine! You will not have him!" As these terrifying words came from nowhere, his face transformed into the ugliest demonic creature imaginable! Now, I had grown up as a Baptist, a cessationist. I had only just begun to walk in the things of the Spirit and consider the supernatural, so I had no knowledge or understanding of situations like this. As he hissed and drooled, lurching towards my face, I got such a terrible fright that instantly I reached for the only weapon available to me, a large NIV Study Bible on my lap, and I smacked him with the most vicious backhanded "Bible-shot" I could muster. The Bible hit him side-on, smashing into his face and then, inexplicably, this large man lifted off the couch, flew and landed on his hands and knees in the middle of the lounge, some two metres from me. Catching our breath, Angus and I watched on in riveted silence as he vomited all over the carpet. This previously aggressive man sobbed in brokenness, which slowly got Angus and me moving. We gently comforted him, and then, with great joy, we prayed with him, and he accepted Jesus as Lord by surrendering his life.

Clive's life continued with many ups and downs, but the experience I had that rainy night with the former Satanist changed my view of the supernatural and the power of the Spirit. I saw first hand how God can use ordinary people, in all their weaknesses. As we sat and chatted that evening, Clive told me that he had tried everything in his power to tear me apart limb from limb, but he was amazed at how, with one hand, I held him firmly in place, my hand resting on his shoulder. He said, "I was bound!" Thank You, Lord. It wasn't to be my last experience of the demonic, but it equipped me in a very, very real way for what was to come. The Christian life is an empowered life. Jesus came to undo the enemy's works, and we are called to do the same. My dreams and expectations took a significant leap after that unusual encounter, and my understanding of God's power underwent a profound transformation. He will be with us to the very end, that's for sure.

Chapter 5

BREAK CAMP AND ADVANCE

It was 1992. With the awakening of our passion for God three years earlier, Heather and I had seen our love for the church, our leadership, and our desire to follow God's purposes grow and grow. Jeff and Viv Kidwell played a constant role in fuelling this ever-increasing passion, drawing us deeper into what would eventually become a lifestyle of abandonment to God and His plan for our lives. Our little family of three had also grown with the arrival of our second son, Richard, some six months earlier. This delightful little boy, with his smile and wispy white hair, brought much joy to us all.

Geopolitically, our nation, South Africa, was on a knife-edge as political leaders juggled the tension of maintaining peace and meeting the expectations of their followers. Nelson Mandela had been freed two years earlier after twenty-seven years of political imprisonment. He was leading the charge towards a free and democratic South Africa, where all races would have an equal say in the nation's future development. Apartheid, as it was known, would soon be a thing of the past, but many obstacles remained to be overcome. White South African voters had recently decisively voted in favour of free and fair elections. Still, even with these massive steps towards equality and dignity for all, violence was never far from us. The far-right threatened harsh consequences, and the far-left a bloodbath if aspirations were not met. Political killings were a regular news item, and uncertainty was a constant in our ever-changing nation. It was in this racially charged atmosphere that the church in our nation slowly started to awaken from its blind or oppressed slumber, both of which had disempowered it.

The tide is turning

Simon Pettit's growing apostolic gift started to play a significant role in reshaping our thinking, and he and others prepared us theologically for what he painted as a very bright and inclusive future. Change was a constant, not only in our nation but also in the church. On the business side, we had also completely restructured the company after my business partnership became untenable. Looking back, I must acknowledge that I carried the primary responsibility for the relational breakdown, as my heart was no longer in it. I longed for something very different from my life, as the church had significantly impacted my worldview. My responses at that time were unformed and immature. I did not know how to navigate the changes happening within my heart. We were forced to sell off the manufacturing side of the business, as well as the main body of the company that managed the franchises. While my brother and I retained the name and product rights for the Western Cape of South Africa, my heart was still not fully in the business world. It all came to a head one afternoon when I received a call from my pastor, Jeff.

"Steve, three of us leaders want to travel to the Southern Drakensberg Mountains to attend a gathering of the NCMI movement of churches. I want to check them out and see how they are doing things. We wondered if you could take a few days off and drive us there. Your Kombi [people carrier] is ideal!" Our newborn, Richard, was now a few months old, but Heather confirmed that she could manage the family, and I should go. I had never been to anything like this before, so I was happy to be "just the driver" and glean as much as I could over the nineteen-hour road trip. The Drakensberg Mountains are a spectacular setting for any event. They tower hundreds of metres above the valleys, and their natural beauty has established them as a protected World Heritage Site. Each section of this chain of mountains has an elaborate name, more of a description, I think, The Amphitheatre, Giant's Castle, Cathedral Peak, to name a few. A large marquee was erected for over two hundred leaders, and we arrived just in time for the evening meal. I was inspired by Dudley Daniels' fervour and the vision that he eloquently laid before us over dinner. He was the leader of this apostolic movement. It was a man's world then; a gathering of tough, can-do-all-things type of leaders, and I must admit to feeling very intimidated and insecure, especially when I didn't know a single person in the room besides Jeff and the two leaders from our church. But God had a purpose.

A captivating story

Collecting my meal from the buffet the next day, I searched the room for a suitable place to sit and noticed a large, bearded man sitting on his own against the window. Plucking up courage, I introduced myself and asked if I could join him; he was most welcoming in his quiet way. His name was Deon Botha, a young Afrikaans-speaking man from the central parts of our country. I was surprised to hear who he was, as he seemed quite different from everyone else in the room. Over lunch, he shared his story that changed my life. He grew up in a very conservative farming community and, like many of his people group, got involved in right-wing politics. He explained how he became a bodyguard for the leader of the Afrikaner Weerstandsbeweging [Afrikaner Resistance Movement], Eugène Terre'Blanche. Following Neo-Nazi practices, they even used a form of the Nazi Swastika as their movement's emblem. But one day, Deon's life radically changed when he encountered Christ and surrendered his life to Him. This decision cost him everything: his position, friendships, farms and even family. He was an outcast. I sat with riveted attention as I witnessed radical devotion to Christ displayed in this young man. He continued to share his story in his thick Afrikaans accent, while handling the English language with great skill. The best was yet to come.

After his radical conversion, Deon received a commission from God to plant churches in Taiwan. As a young, single Afrikaans man, he travelled to Taiwan and founded the ministry. While learning the language and getting to know the people in a remote area of the nation (if my memory serves me well), Deon wrote to his childhood sweetheart, asked her to marry him, and explained that it would likely cost her family. She would have to settle for a life in the nations, specifically the Far East. He smiled as he shared what a wonderful invitation it was, and it captivated my attention. He went on to tell me that she travelled to Taiwan, where they married and, together, they set their course in Christ. He was a truly beautiful man. Not once did his story point to anything else but Jesus. It was a life-shaping moment for me.

With my heart significantly softened by the encounter with Deon, I joined all the gathered leaders for the week's first session. The worship was incredibly inspiring, mainly because it carried the movement's message, which was "a call to the nations". When Dudley Daniels took to the platform, he asked us to open our Bibles to the book of Deuteronomy, specifically to chapter one. As I was merely the driver, I sat at the back but decided to take notes in a small exercise book I found at the local store. The energy and devotion in the room for their task were electrifying, and I found it tremendously inspiring. Dudley explained the passage's context and how the Israelites had settled at Mount Sinai three months after leaving Egypt. Following God's instruction, approximately two million Israelites set up camp at the base of the mountain, which must have been a welcome break after months of wandering across Sinai. But then, after some eight or nine months, came the word of the Lord to his people: "You have camped at this mountain long enough; break camp and advance!" I was captivated by this message, hanging on every word, which made total sense to me. I can imagine how the Israelites would have established themselves at the mountain, settling, perhaps planting seeds, setting up routines, and being in awe of everything that took place there. It was costly for them to break camp. I could see that.

Dudley Daniels then spoke to his leaders and said, "We, too, NCMI, have camped at this mountain of togetherness [South Africa] too long. It is time we break camp and advance into the nations!" I'm not sure how many churches were represented in that tent that day, but many years later, NCMI was able to speak of over three thousand church plants across the world because of that message in the Drakensberg; what a message, and what a reward for their obedience!

Ruined for mission

As Dudley Daniels brought his prophetic message to a close, he shared that he was convinced that there were men and women in the tent who were hearing the call "to break camp and advance"! He encouraged those feeling God's call to come to the front, and without hesitation, I was one of the first on the move, all the way from the back. My heart was pounding; I was responding to a new purpose for my life, and nothing was going to deter me from God's clear calling. I fixed my eyes on the front and strode forward, not wanting to make eye contact with Jeff Kidwell, just in case I, the driver, wasn't allowed to do what I was doing. I received prayer from some of the leadership team and felt such confirmation in my heart that Heather and I needed to begin "breaking camp" and preparing ourselves for advance. Thus, a heart journey began. Some would say I was "ruined for mission" that day, and I guess I was.

We are going to the nations!

The nineteen-hour journey home was charged with excitement as we processed all that had happened to us. I was invigorated by the experience, and on returning home to Heather, I announced with great excitement as I entered the front door, "We're going to the nations!" Understandably, a somewhat tired mother passed me our new baby, Richard, and said, "Well, start with him, and then you'd better tell me all about it!" Praise God for Heather; God had given me just the right person for this great adventure, and over the years she would prove her unbelievable capacity for God's purposes, time and time again, and this was to be one of our strengths. On numerous occasions over the years, Heather would tell me, "I am the last person on earth who should be doing this!" However, each time, she would respond positively and enthusiastically to God's call. Amazing.

Our excitement was further fuelled when Jeff and Viv asked to see us late one afternoon. Sharing confidentially, Jeff told us that The Vineyard Fellowship, under Simon's leadership, would undergo a transformation from what it had been known for. Firstly, the Vineyard movement in the USA asked if we would be willing to change our church's name to alleviate confusion and allow them to establish new churches in South Africa. So, a name change to Jubilee Church Cape Town was imminent. Furthermore, Simon was finding it difficult to have the church spread all over the peninsula and wanted to pull all five congregations together for a season to shape the church's values and vision. However, there was one problem: one of the communities was quite far away, and the leaders felt that it would be difficult for them to participate in a meaningful way with the new structure due to the distance. After much prayer and discussion among the leaders, Simon suggested that Jeff and Viv take this remote congregation and plant an autonomous church in Muizenberg, a suburb some forty kilometres from the city centre. Both Jeff and Viv shared how they had been considering this for some time, and now, having confirmed the call of God, they gave their confirmation to the rest of the team at The Vineyard, soon to be called Jubilee Church.

Birth of The Bay Community Church

"Steve, Heather, we want you to come with us and help plant this church! We've spoken to Simon, and he is happy for us to join Clark, Karen, Mac, and Adien for this new plant. Will you come?" The "big ask" that day transformed our world, and for the first time, I had a front-row seat in a church-planting context and in church leadership. Like new parents preparing for the birth of their first child, we could speak about nothing else; the excitement was tangible. The Bay Community Church, located in Muizenberg, was established a year later, in 1993.

Those early days of the new church were a lot of fun. Jeff created an infectious atmosphere of expectation, filled with a longing for the presence of the Lord. Small beginnings soon led to rapid growth, but never at the cost of our experiencing God, and Jeff made sure of that. In those early days, I learnt to rely on God to change individual lives through prayer and the laying on of hands. We spent Sunday evenings at "River Meetings", where we would gather to worship God, pray for one another, and soak in His presence. All of this was preparation for the things to come, something I would always be grateful for. I also had the privilege of working closely with Clark Ellis and Mac Oosthuizen, who were extremely gifted in their leadership ability, and they, too, shaped my life as we worked as a team. I have incredibly fond memories of those Bay days!

God was on the move, and we knew it. Even as our nation was shaken by many incidents during those days leading up to our very first free elections planned for April 1994, like the assassination of political activist and leader Chris Hani, the bombing of St James Church in Kenilworth, Cape Town, and deep divisions that raged between the political groups due to tribal leanings, leading to riots and many unnecessary killings. All these took centre stage in the news, but in the background, God was at work in His church! Word began to spread about an unusual move of God following Rodney Howard Browne's ministry in the USA. Particularly, a church in Toronto, Canada, spoke of an outpouring that brought great refreshing to many and continued night after night. Our hunger to know and experience this kind of Holy Spirit refreshing grew.

Chapter 6

ENCOUNTER

For any of the twenty-plus million South Africans who joined the queues to vote in the first free election on 27th April 1994, it will be a day forever etched in their memory. After forty-six years of Apartheid (Policy of Separate Development), all South Africans had the chance to vote, and the atmosphere of the occasion was beyond description. Previously separated by race, skin colour, and opportunity, the new South Africa came together in a day of togetherness never seen among us. There was a memorable and grand celebration. Gone were the fears of a possible civil war or the significant disruption to our society that many had spoken of. All we saw and experienced was joy and togetherness. In the queues that stretched over one kilometre in places, sweets, drinks, and foodstuffs were freely shared, adding to the party-like atmosphere on that momentous day. No one was in a rush or inconvenienced, as we all enjoyed the historic moment.

We are a rainbow nation

There were countless stories of God breaking in at critical times and accounts of many prayers being answered. In one incident, a key political figure walked out of the final negotiations, declaring that he and his large political party would not participate in the upcoming elections. He promptly boarded a flight back to his city, only for the plane to break down on the runway a few minutes later. He was forced to return to the terminal building, where he was once again reunited with the negotiators. In this unusual setting, a final agreement was reached, allowing the elections to proceed as planned. The aircraft carrying this key political figure then departed without a hitch. We were part of a miracle, and we knew it! Archbishop Desmond Tutu, a vocal figure in those decisive days, coined the phrase, "We're a rainbow nation", and it became a household term to describe what we were all seeing and experiencing. Post-election, our new president, Nelson Mandela, stated, "The new South Africa is a rainbow nation at peace with itself and the world." Over eighty-six per cent of the registered voters ensured we all enjoyed the miracle that day. A new South Africa had been born.

The Toronto blessing

These were new days in our nation and new days of opportunity for the church as well. Something truly significant was happening in the church, not only in South Africa but also worldwide. Whatever gathering one went to, people were talking about it. Stories emerged of a strange but powerful move of God in Mississauga, Toronto, Canada, that first occurred in the middle of April 1994, just as we were preparing to vote for change in South Africa. From what we heard during an evening meeting, spontaneous and unexpected joy had been poured out on the congregation, spreading uncontrollably throughout the room. The preacher, Randy Clarke from the USA, didn't quite know what to do with it. Should he keep preaching? Call for order? However, as the meeting proceeded, individuals started to share how inexpressible love and joy had filled their hearts. They wanted to worship and pray, and no one wanted to leave the meeting! And so, what was born became known as The Toronto Blessing, as it continued night after night. Not everyone embraced it, and immediately, some people took their stand against it, deeply dividing Christian communities at times. Those opposed circulated stories of abuses and excesses, pointing to the dishonouring of the preaching of the Word. At the same time, those embracing this fresh outpouring shared about life-changing encounters and a new fruitfulness in their Christian walk. For us in The Bay Community Church, Muizenberg, Cape Town, there was only one real response: to dive right in! Through Jeff and Viv Kidwell's ministry in the church, we had been nurtured in an environment of the Holy Spirit, continually being encouraged to allow the presence of God to invade every space of our hearts. It was the defining atmosphere of this young church, responding to a desire to be "a well of refreshing" to all who would come.

Information about what was happening in Toronto was scarce to begin with, but one thing was sure: something quite different was happening. Meetings continued daily, with some sessions held twice a day, and the number of attendees was increasing. There were many accounts of significant healing and lives being transformed in the unusual presence of the Holy Spirit. The usual two-hour meetings stretched well into the night, and nobody wanted to go home. Long queues formed well before the meetings began and attendance numbers had to be limited. A great revival was spreading in this small community close to Toronto International Airport in Canada. During those heady days, we loved hearing any snippet of news passed on through photocopies of articles, testimonies, and stories that circulated. Our local community would gather early each Tuesday morning for an hour or so of prayer. We had done this well before the church plant, and it was a time we all loved, even on the cold winter mornings that Cape Town often delivered.

One morning, God moved powerfully among us and one could sense the intensity of what God was doing. All I remember was being thrown backwards as a "wave of blessing" passed through the room. Sadly, one of our plastic chairs got in the way and disintegrated beneath me. I understand I still have an outstanding bill at The Bay Community Church! At that moment, God impressed upon my heart that I would soon be going to Toronto and would experience Him in a new way. I casually shared this with those who gathered for prayer as we ended our time together, not fully understanding the details or the implications.

New York, New York

Shortly after receiving this prophetic word, a business associate, Jan Molenaar, asked if I would travel with him to a trade fair in New York, USA. With South Africa opening to the world post-Apartheid, we felt it was time to consider new product ranges and investigate whether there was a market for our locally designed and manufactured products.

So, early in October 1994, Jan and I headed to the USA to attend a ten-day Electronic Security exhibition at the World Trade Centre in New York. Jan was a marvellous travelling companion, full of fun, and we enjoyed the great expanse of the trade fair and the excitement of all New York had to offer. For days, we experienced all we could and walked the length and breadth of that great city. The weather was equally kind, and we enjoyed every moment of our time together. To our surprise, we discovered that the trade fair would close for four days due to the Columbus Day holiday weekend. Jan and I considered how we would use the time: to travel to Disney World or stay in the city? There were so many options, but one took me totally by surprise.

Re-route to Toronto

Early in the morning, I was enjoying God in my personal prayer time when I was "arrested" by the presence of God. These times are very personal and hard to put into words, but it was a real experience of God filling the room, and I couldn't move. With it came the instruction, "You must go to Toronto." I was overwhelmed with excitement and anticipation, and even though I would need to get a visa and airline ticket, I knew I was going! Breakfast with Jan was a little tense. My announcement that I would leave him in New York and head across to Toronto for a "church gathering" was a little hard for him to hear. "Why? We're having so much fun! Church? Seriously?" he said. I was so convinced that God had spoken, and I stood my ground. Jan relented, and I spent the rest of the day arranging my travel plans and visa. On Friday 7th October 1994, I arrived in Mississauga, Toronto.

It was about two miles from my hotel along Dixie Street to the Airport Vineyard Church in Mississauga, Toronto. I set off early and arranged a taxi to take me to the church facility. On arrival, I was shocked to find a long queue stretching the length of the building. I took my place and waited patiently for the doors to open. People queuing to go to church was a first-time experience for me! I was captivated by the buzz of excitement in the queue as I listened to stories of what had been happening to those attending the meetings. The expectation was alive and electric, and it wasn't hard to be caught up in the excitement of the occasion. The queue grew and grew behind us. The buzz among the crowd also grew. It wasn't too long before the doors opened and we slowly filed into quite a small space, no more than enough room for some four hundred adults. I was immediately struck by the friendliness and simplicity of the people, especially those who called this their spiritual home. When one hears of the great moves of God, one's imagination can get clouded by all sorts of false impressions of what it may look and feel like. What I was witnessing was very ordinary, with no hype.

I enjoyed the worship, although I admit to being a spectator, trying to absorb as much as I could. I can, however, remember being captivated by a song which spoke of the streets of heaven being golden, such a captivating invitation. It is such a great melody and so full of tremendous promise! Then John Arnott, the leader of the church, brought a heart-melting message about the Father-heart of God. His large frame, dulcet tones, and winsome ways exemplified the message as he drew us into the presence of a loving Father and His willingness to bless us. Spontaneous laughter erupted through the message as individuals enjoyed the unusual presence in the room. To my surprise, John ignored them as if it were quite usual and pressed on. Then came the invitation for prayer.

The large crowd was given strict instructions on how the prayer ministry would be administered. After the chairs were removed, we were instructed to stand on the areas marked by lines on the floor to receive prayer ministry. I took my place, heart beating with expectation. I received prayer a few times that evening and, each time, the overpowering presence of God left me unable to stand, resulting in a lengthy period of "carpet time" (lying down on the floor). I returned to my hotel just before midnight. Lying in bed that evening, I processed what I had seen and experienced. Was this any different from what we were experiencing at my home church? Had I come all this way to be a "spiritual tourist", something I detest? I was slightly confused, and even a slight disappointment gripped my heart. I had expected more.

The following morning, I joined a growing number of church leaders for a "Pastors' Morning", where John Arnott gave us some insight into what he believed was taking place and how it should be encouraged. He walked us through Scripture and provided biblical examples of times when individuals were seemingly overwhelmed by encountering God. Many questions followed, and he gave us his best explanation. Quite understandably, some aspects were a mystery! I was very impressed by his humility and grace when questions got a little controversial or sharp.

Not being a pastor myself, I kept a very low profile but enjoyed the insight into the mighty change that would occur if the church embraced this move of God. One of the most common questions among the leaders was how to manage a move of God like this one. What happens if I lose people? How do we know what is of God and what is just a distraction? Questions like these came quickly, and John Arnott's answers deeply impacted me as he pastored the pastors. What was clear was that God was doing something fresh.

Once again, the room was cleared of all chairs and other obstacles, and space was made to begin praying for these leaders. I found a quiet spot at the back of the hall, as I was not a pastor. However, I was prayed for and, once again, the overwhelming presence of God had a profound impact on my heart. After the meeting, we were invited to the home of a church member to enjoy the company of a local family and experience some excellent hospitality. I enjoyed the afternoon of fellowship and was a bit taken aback when I was offered a Bear Paw Burger! My host smiled widely as he explained that it wasn't a bear paw, but a beef-burger equivalent to the size of a very large bear paw! He was right; it was massive! The afternoon allowed me to meet other visitors to Toronto and listen to some incredible stories from across the nations. At this time, I began to feel incredibly homesick and very far away from Heather and our two little boys back home in Cape Town, South Africa.

Later that afternoon, I was dropped off at my hotel and homesickness came over me like a flood. It was so intense that I picked up the phone and called American Airlines to see if they could reschedule my flight and get me back to New York that evening. The lines were jam-packed, and I was put on hold, where I had to endure the repetitive sound of the chirpy on-hold music, regularly punctuated by advertisements. During this long, noisy wait, a small, quiet voice spoke into my heart. "Where are you going? I'm not finished with you yet." I knew God had spoken, and just then, a cheerful American Airlines voice began to ask how she could help me. I declared, "I've had a change of heart and plans!" promptly disconnecting the call. I ran across the room, picked up my coat and rushed out the door, knowing that the evening meeting was just about to begin, and was two kilometres away. I remember running like Elijah ran before the rain! There was no time to wait for a taxi. I had to run. Hurrying into the meeting hall, I noticed the room was already packed, and I was ushered to a space in the far left-hand corner. Something had shifted in my heart.

The evening was filled with the most wonderful worship. John Arnott encouraged us in the Word, and my hunger and thirst for God's purposes grew and grew. We took our places on the marked-out carpet as the invitation was given for those who would like to be prayed over. During prayer time, I decided to try to beat the system. Making full use of my long legs, I began to slowly edge forward, row by row, so that I could receive prayer from none other than John Arnott himself, who was praying for individuals way down at the front. At various intervals, I received prayers from different people, but I managed to hold myself together, with the front row clearly in mind. I remember that the journey to the front took two hours! I don't know how I managed it, but I was successful and soon found myself in row three. I would have reached my objective with only two more rows to go. But God had other plans.

Big things come in small packages!

A small but commanding voice suddenly interrupted my progress: "Would you like prayer?" I looked down, and there before me was an extremely diminutive woman who had introduced herself as one of the children's workers in the church. A children's worker? I will not reveal all the uncharitable thoughts that went through my proud heart at that moment, but I realised that I was going nowhere without her praying for me; the expression on her face made that clear. I submitted, resolving that after she had prayed for me, even though it was now 10:45 p.m., I would continue my quest to reach John Arnott himself. Reaching as high as she could to lay a hand on my forehead, she began to pray: "Lord, bless this man."

With this simple prayer came the power of God with such intensity that it kept me on the floor for the next four hours, allowing me to eventually return to my hotel room only at 3:20 a.m. in the wee hours of the following morning. As you can imagine, this changed my attitude towards children's workers for the rest of my life. That simple prayer marked the beginning of a life-transforming experience.

Chapter 7

A CHANGE OF HEART

Carpet time in Toronto

For more than four hours, I experienced God in a way I had never before. I can remember weeping, then sobbing, feeling as if my heart was being ripped out and that my chest cavity was fully exposed. I became aware of a growing number of people gathered around me, praying quietly and offering their support during this time. I was also mindful of the closeness to God Himself and felt so small, insignificant, and broken. During this extraordinary encounter, God began to reveal things to me.

Heart surgery

At one point in this dramatic experience, I saw my heart placed before me as if it had been removed from my ribcage and put on full display for all to see. It was a large mass, which I instantly identified as the essence of my identity. The moment I saw it, I wept because it was covered in deep scars. It looked like a meat-clever had been let loose on it; what a mess. Life's experiences can leave lasting damage, as we know; they can shape us, hold us back, and inhibit us if they are not addressed. The apostle Paul called them strongholds. In His love and grace, God began to show me, one by one, what each of the scars represented.

One of life's incidents that scarred me was my mother's illness. As referenced earlier in this account, in 1987, I witnessed the decline and death of my mother due to lymphoma cancer. It was a terrible experience as we were very close, and, to add to it, I was not walking with God at the time. Watching her fade away in immense pain left me very angry with God and emotionally locked up. Not being able to add much value to those last days of my mother's life left me feeling like a failure. As I encountered this scar before me, God gave me the most wonderful gift and freeing vision. It was of my "resurrected" mother, Maureen, in all her beauty, free of sickness and suffering, glowing, full of life and in the presence of her loving God. In her final days, she encountered Jesus in a very real and assuring way. She was a magnificent sight, and as I gazed at this incredible vision, I noticed that one of the scars in my large, messy heart began to fade away until it was no longer visible. It was healed and dealt with.

Tears of distress and pain turned to tears of joy as healing flooded my life. But very soon, I was taken to the next scar, which was the second of five scars that God was to take me through. With each experience, I watched as the scars vanished before my eyes, and my heart was made whole. To use the words of Paul, the strongholds were demolished! I know men carry a lot of pain, but I never realised that men had so many tears. Through all this time, my faithful children's worker and her team never left my side, demonstrating their outstanding servant hearts. It was well into the early morning hours when the tears finally subsided, and I became more aware of what was happening around me. The lightness in my heart, the joy of being free, and the very presence of God were overwhelming, and suddenly, I could laugh again.

I wish I could remember the name of that kind lady who gave up her night to minister to me. How I would have loved to share all that with her, what I have gone on to become and do: the better husband I have become, the more present father I have become, the churches I have planted, and the nations I have reached! As I regained a measure of dignity, she leaned forward and, in her quiet, confident voice, said: "I want to break some things over your life." She continued and asked God to take away the fear of man that had so limited and humiliated me all my life. I was surprised she knew about it, because I thought it was well hidden. But with her simple prayer came another powerful, chain-smashing experience where I felt my inner man was being ripped out once again. "There you go," she said, "now I can go home. Good night." And, with a sweet goodbye, off she went.

The daisies of Africa!

I lay on that floor for some time, trying to process all that I had experienced when I was tapped on the shoulder. I rolled onto my side to see who was trying to catch my attention. To my surprise, it was one of the other guests that I had met at the barbecue earlier that afternoon. His name was Chris Light, and he was from Manchester, England. I had loved listening to his story earlier that day, and we had struck up a friendship. He apologised to me, knowing that he was not supposed to minister to another visitor, but he felt sure that God had given him a word for me, and if I were happy, he would like to share it with me. I was in no place to argue with anyone, so I just smiled appreciatively. Little did I know that I was just about to receive a prophetic word that would shape the rest of my life and that of my family, commissioning us for the future. Chris quietly prophesied.

> "The Lord says, I am sending you to the daisies of Africa – a people who are many and a people who are without hope. You are to go! Go take hope to the hopeless."

In the early morning hours, I slowly made my way to the exit of the Dixie Road venue. I was surprised to see how many people still lingered, enjoying God's presence. As I reached the main exit, I finally had the opportunity to meet John Arnott, the leader of the church. "You've had a good evening!" he said with a friendly, wry smile. "Life-changing!" I said. Picking up my strange accent, John asked where I was from, and I told him I was from Cape Town, South Africa. He placed his hands on my head and prayed, "Go bless Africa!" What generous people they were! No wonder God entrusted them with such a rich blessing.

Filled with much of the presence of God, I left, carrying those words of John Arnott and the feeling of those hands of blessing. That's exactly what I wanted to do. It was 3:20 a.m.!

Whenever I read the story of the lame beggar positioned at the temple gates in the early parts of Acts in the Bible and see how Peter and John give him more than he ever expected, it reminds me of all that happened to me in Toronto in 1994. When the apostle Peter explains to the crowd that gathered because of that incredible miracle, he explains that "faith . . . through Jesus has given the man this perfect health" (Acts 3:16 ESV). This man's *perfect health* can also be translated as *complete wholeness,* i.e. he didn't only get restored legs, but it seems God healed him internally as well, dealing with the shame, loss of dignity and isolation that would have plagued him for years, besides the creative miracle of a pair of new legs! Imagine the distress of being carried daily to the gates to beg. Now healed, he is at the centre of things, enjoying his "wholeness", and one could confidently imagine his life was never the same again. I wonder how many times he got to tell his story about the wonderful grace of God and of Peter and John standing before the Sanhedrin and seeing their horror at not being able to hide the facts of this unusual miracle.

Looking back, I can see the correlation between those healing moments on the floor in Toronto and what God has released me into over the years. Would it have been possible if God had not made me whole? In my case, each of the deep scars had resulted from some form of traumatic experience. In his excellent book *Demolishing Strongholds*, David Devenish explains that Paul uses the analogy of building a defensive stronghold within a walled city to keep an invader out. He writes:

> *"I believe that many people come to Christ, give their lives to Him, and in that sense, the outer wall of their life is taken. However, the stronghold is not taken, and that stronghold represents a way of thinking from before the time they were saved. It will have*

been influenced by their culture, their past sins, their upbringing, experiences, and events that have happened to them. In other words, they are Christians, but in their deepest thinking, they are still influenced by strongholds of the enemy."[2]

That would describe me before this experience of the Spirit. Trauma and many bad decisions had left me scarred. God had ministered to me through His church by His grace, and I came out of that time a very different person. I'm so grateful for the Spirit's work in me, those dear friends in the Airport Vineyard Church, and the hours they knelt by me. I wonder if we give enough attention to serving one another in this way?

---

2. David Devenish, *Demolishing Strongholds: Effective Strategies for Spiritual Warfare* (Authentic Media, 2013).

Chapter 8

MAN OF PEACE

After my extended time in the USA, Heather (who was now three months pregnant with our third child) and I decided it was time to take a break from the busyness of my work and travels. We left Cape Town and started the fourteen-hour journey to one of our favourite places in South Africa, the Eastern Free State, to the Sunnyside Guest Farm. This beautiful farm is just outside the little town of Clarens. We call it a town, but at the time, there was not much besides a large Dutch Reformed Church for the local farming families, a municipal office building, a general dealer and a few small homes scattered across a hill. Clarens was named after the town in Switzerland where the Boer War commandos' leader, Paul Kruger, was eventually exiled in 1902 after the war. At the time, nothing indicated that it would ever become the town it is today. Our long journey to this place always had a sense of excitement, as we loved the area and Sunnyside Guest Farm, with its quaint chalets, delicious farm meals, and stunning scenery. It was the sort of place where rest and recuperation were guaranteed.

Heather, our two young sons, Cameron and Richard, and I strolled along the gravel road that passes the upper Sunnyside Basotho village and wound our way down the hill back to the guest farm nestled among the trees in the valley below. The late afternoon light in the Golden Gate Valley is often called the "golden hour", as the evening light brings out the array of spectacular colours in the surrounding mountains and sandstone buttresses. As we slowly meandered along the road, it was here that life took an unexpected and sudden turn as God spoke.

When entering this Golden Gate Valley in the Eastern Free State, one is immediately struck by the magnificence of the large, earth-coloured sandstone buttresses that stand proudly above the valley. It is such an unusual sight in South Africa, and one can understand why these majestic edifices carry names like The Sentinel or Face Rock. There are very few indigenous trees in these savannah grasslands, except for willows and poplars introduced by the early European settlers, mainly as dowries for future weddings. *Ouhout* (Old wood), an exception, is one of the very few trees found in abundance, and it lines the valleys and mountainsides with its flaky bark that gives the impression that it is much older than it is. These beautiful surroundings were to be the backdrop, like an artist's canvas, for the outworking of God's purposes in Heather's life and mine. It was here that the *Daisies of Africa* awaited.

Childhood memories

My fondness for the area grew from my blossoming romance with Heather. Early in our relationship, Heather's father, Mike, told me, "If you are going to have a serious relationship with Heather, you will have to love the Eastern Free State!" I didn't fully understand what he meant, or even where it was, until my first visit with the family in 1982, the year we got married. I soon discovered that Sunnyside Guest Farm was a beautiful place and played an enormous part in Heather's childhood memories. Over the first few days of arriving there, Heather took me to every spot that had held a fond memory for her. She had naughtily scratched her name in the cave on the mountainside.

Hopelessly in love

Her father, Mike, and his younger brother, David, had spent two years of their life at Sunnyside Farm during the 1940s, when they were approximately ten and twelve years of age, respectively. These were difficult days for their family, but Mike often spoke of those times as the best years of his life, which resulted in him maintaining a close bond with the guest farm that Ann and Dennis Boland eventually took over. Heather would often recount stories of her annual trips back to Sunnyside as a child, including tales of locust swarms, snowfall so deep at times that one couldn't walk around, baboons, and many other wonderful memories. And now, since my first visit to the Free State in 1982, it didn't take long before I fell hopelessly in love with these valleys, the mountains, and all they had to offer.

In 1994, twelve years later, here we were walking along these familiar roads with our two little boys in the late afternoon sunshine. As we enjoyed the surroundings, my experiences in Toronto ten days prior were never far from my mind. I could still sense God's deep work in my life and the feeling of being "plugged in". There is no easy way to describe the closeness of the Spirit of God during those days. Just as we were about to enter the Sunnyside gates, God spoke. Looking back, I guess, it was the very first time I ever felt that I "heard" the voice of God.

"I want you to take the gospel to Japela"

At first, I thought Heather might have heard it too, but when she said she hadn't, I immediately told her what had just happened. I was stunned and didn't know what to make of it. Japela Semaase was a seventy-year-old Basotho man who was both a friend and the headman of the local Basotho people. To the young men, he was fearsome. For us, he was a mystical man, full of fascinating stories, and, sadly, he displayed a deep subservient humility, having grown up in the Apartheid years. He often accompanied us when we hiked to the top of Langkraans or Angel's Wing Mountains, which surrounded the farm, acting as our guide and storyteller. Lunch breaks on the hike would often be taken up with him telling us intriguing stories of his childhood when he had lived in the mountains for weeks on end, erecting the barbed-wire fences that separated the farms. One of our favourite stories was about how he and other young boys would "run down a buck", a mountain antelope. The Mountain Rhebok is a beautiful animal that is very nimble and fast over a short distance. But when young, fit, inexhaustible Basotho men continue to pursue it over long distances, it finally collapses and is captured for the evening pot! The chase would last for hours at times. Quite extraordinary! In other stories, he recounted tales of soldiers returning on horseback from the two world wars, while families and farm labourers lined the gravel roads with great shouts and celebration. At times, it felt as if he had been alive forever! We loved Japela and his stories.

Now that I knew God had spoken, I didn't know what to do with it. Nothing like this had ever happened to me before, and, in the past, I would have dismissed it due to my fear of man. Fear of rejection can be a powerful enemy if not overcome. But now things were different. It was clear that God had dealt with that issue while I was on the floor in Toronto. Here was my first chance for God's healing to be put to the test! Silently, I shuddered inside. I shared how I felt with Heather and, quite confidently, she said, "You must go then!" It sounded so simple, but the truth was, I had never shared the gospel in that sort of context before. Where would I start? What if Japela didn't want to listen? I wasn't sure I knew all the Scriptures! What if he asked me questions I couldn't answer? My mind buzzed with the many unknowns as we silently returned to our chalet at the guest farm. Nevertheless, I went the next day.

Japela

Japela's village was a ten-minute walk down the valley. At four o'clock the next afternoon, I took my Bible and fuelled up with nervous prayers, headed off with great support from Heather. I can remember that walk as if it were yesterday. As I made my way, doubts and personal issues began to give way to pioneering joy. It was all a little surreal. In a sense, I felt strangely at home doing this, as though it were the most natural thing in the world. The afternoon hush had settled over the village, and the familiar smell of the dry willow wood burning on the evening fires was comforting. It was a beautiful evening, and it was hard not to be absorbed into the vista that stretched before me. To my delight, I arrived at Japela's little mud-and-thatch house and found him sitting on the customary mud step surrounding each home. There he sat, his woolly cap pulled down over his ears, his Basotho blanket wrapped tightly around his shoulders and his stick, with baboon tail-hairs on the end, firmly in his hand. The headman's stance was so simple. His eyes widened when I startled him by appearing around the corner, but his face immediately broke into a broad, welcoming smile. He couldn't rise from his place and apologised profusely. He explained that his legs had little strength lately and found getting up nearly impossible, so he spent much time sitting in this quiet spot. I asked if I could join him on the step, and he happily obliged, as we exchanged the customary handshake and chatted for a while about the beauty of the valley and the mountains that lay before us, soaking in the late afternoon sun. The view from his front step was breathtakingly beautiful. As we sat, I realised that the next problem to overcome was language! Japela couldn't speak English, and I did not understand his beautiful mother tongue, Sesotho. We laughed our way into our best-shared language, Afrikaans.

After a short time of small talk, I asked Japela how he was. His response still rings in my ears: "*Kleinbaas,* I am not well. I am worried that I am soon to die, and I don't know where I am going." (*Kleinbaas* was a subservient term used for white people by the farm labourers in the days of Apartheid, which means, "young-Master". It took me three years or so to get Japela to call me Steve, but when he finally managed to do it, he laughed for a long time. That was a truly memorable moment!) Japela's response to my question was a fantastic opening to why I had visited him. Isn't God so gracious? I began to tell him about the Lord Jesus and how He was the One who had created the mountains and valleys that lay before us. I felt the conversation flow smoothly until he asked, "But isn't He only the God of the white man? I was told he wasn't for us?"

My first daisy!

What an indictment against our so-called "white Christian nation"! From Genesis, I explained that God had created all men equal and that He had sent His Son, Jesus, to rescue all people from the consequences of sin, fear, shame, and separation from God Himself. Japela needed no explanation of his sinful inner state. Constantly referring to the creation around us, I could explain that Jesus had come for him, too, *Ntate* Japela. (*Ntate* means "father", a term of respect when speaking to an older man.) Such was the trust of this dear, older man that he seemed immediately satisfied with my answer and, obviously, God was doing a deep work in his heart. Right then and there, with simple faith, he accepted this new revelation that he, too, was included. I watched as the truth and weight of the gospel penetrated the depths of this dear man's heart. Quietly yet sincerely, and with great confidence, Japela told me that he, too, wanted Jesus as his Lord and that he yearned for the assurance of eternity promised by the gospel. I explained how this happens by declaring faith in Jesus Christ, acknowledging sins and being forgiven, and slowly, he followed the words of my simple Afrikaans prayer. There, on the step of his simple home, Japela Semaase became a child of God! I'm not sure I can fully recall or explain all the emotions that flooded my heart and head at that moment, but I remember the deep rumble of his quiet laughter as we hugged and celebrated together, and I know that all of heaven rejoiced, too! To this day, I have never seen someone's physical appearance change so dramatically at the time of salvation. Japela's face transformed before me, and we embraced together on that little mud step.

When Peter, at Pentecost, declared the purposes of God to the crowds in Jerusalem, he made it quite clear what was needed. He called for repentance, a "complete turning-around", and instructed all to be baptised as a sign of their new faith. As we know, many responded on that day. Later, when asked to explain how the lame man of some forty years had been healed, Peter explained it is "the faith which comes through Him [Jesus] has given him this . . . complete wholeness in your presence" (Acts 3:16 AMP). Within God's mighty rescue plan is the promise of wholeness. With the new confidence I had, I told Japela about this and said, "Let us now pray for your healing!"

I placed one hand on his neck and another on his weak limbs and asked God to heal him and raise him. He did! Japela quickly stood, stretching his legs one at a time. He chuckled as he discovered that strength had returned, and he was filled with joy. With much laughter and a lightness of spirit, he joined me, and we walked back towards the farmhouses where we were staying. Japela was a new man! With more hugs, I said goodbye and promised to bring Heather back the following afternoon to visit and talk more about Jesus. He was delighted that we would come to his home, something uncommon in those days of racial division.

One look at me was enough to tell Heather something very significant had happened, and after giving her a complete account of all that had taken place, she couldn't wait to see Japela for herself. Unbeknown to us, Japela began sharing what had happened with his elderly wife, Polly. Polly was a dear, elderly Basotho lady who outwardly displayed the hardships of village life and the years she had spent struggling to survive in extreme poverty. Her hands told the story of many years of hard work. When Japela entered the front door, Polly was surprised by how he had walked so confidently towards her now that God's healing power had done its work. In his simple understanding of the gospel, he told her all that had happened, and he was able to lead Polly through the same simple prayer that he had just prayed thirty minutes before. The gospel had come to this little "ethnos" or "clan", just as God had promised Abraham, Isaac, and Jacob it would do.

The next day, Heather and I left the boys under the care of others and headed down to the Sunnyside labourers' village. We were still a way off when a smiling Japela greeted us from afar. The embrace was warm and full of understanding, reflecting a shared oneness in our faith. He escorted us down to his house, where we found an equally radiant Polly! We were taken aback when Japela explained that she, too, had received Jesus! It was obvious to Heather and me as their faces were radiant with new life. After some casual conversation, limited by language difficulties, we prayed for them, hugged, and laughed, finding it difficult to find the right words to describe what we had witnessed. It was with mixed emotions of joy and sadness that we bid them farewell and returned to the cottage to pack for our return trip to Cape Town the following morning. On the fourteen-hour journey, we marvelled at what had taken place and God's amazing grace that reaches the most "insignificant" in the world's eyes. The gospel is truly *good news for the poor*.

The beginning of a God story

A few weeks before, I had been on the floor during a meeting in Toronto, and my life and world was turned upside down. Amid that life-changing experience, a prophetic word came that would become a way of life for Heather, the boys and me: *"I am sending you to the daisies of Africa . . ."* What we didn't know on that journey home was that God had given us our first *"daisies"*. Japela had become a *"man of peace"*, someone who would welcome us into his community and become a door to reach a nation, just as Jesus had described to His disciples when He sent them out to the surrounding towns and villages with good news. "Look for someone who will welcome you in." We had found someone just like that. A God story had begun, and we were blissfully unaware of the part we were about to play. We returned home to what we believed would be "back to normal" – but it wasn't to be.

Chapter 9

THE PEOPLE ARE WAITING

The Holy Spirit moved powerfully across the wider charismatic church in late 1994 and 1995. No matter what occasion or meeting one attended, there would be a flow of the Spirit, which brought tremendous hunger and expectation for God and His purposes within the church. As our family returned to Cape Town after our eventful time in the Eastern Free State, we continued to be immensely encouraged by Japela and Polly's recent commitment to Christ. We shared this remarkable story far and wide, inspiring others. The story of my visit to the Airport Vineyard in Toronto also spread, and I got my first taste of public ministry as I was asked to share it in several different contexts.

Our newly planted church in Muizenberg, The Bay Community Church, prospered, and we welcomed many new families. On occasions, God would move so sovereignly among us that there would be no opportunity to bring the Word, quite something for believers who loved the Word of God. The church soaked up all that God was doing, and lives were transformed. At one Sunday morning meeting, I found myself praying for a new couple who had recently joined us, and as I prayed for them, I felt God say to me, "You will work closely with this man in the years to come." I shared this with Peter Bonney boldly, not knowing what it meant. Those were such unusual times, and it's a joy to look back and see how Peter and Janis Bonney, along with their family, moved to join us in the Free State a few years later, becoming an integral part of the work that continues to this day.

Having personally read many accounts of the early revivals, we counted ourselves very privileged to be experiencing God in this new way and seeing such fruitfulness awakened in individuals' lives right across the church. At the time, we didn't know that this move of God activated more new church plants than ever seen in a revival context in history. With many people unlocked by the Spirit's work in their hearts, leaders found new courage to step out and plant new communities of the Spirit, and these were exhilarating times.

Training for eldership

As we stepped into 1995, Jeff Kidwell and Simon Pettit began training Mac Oosthuyzen, Clark Ellis, and me for eldership in The Bay Community Church. It was a tremendous honour, and I relished every opportunity to grow in God and leadership.

The genuine understanding of servant leadership we embraced as churches was a shaping time for me. I loved the church and loved serving the leaders God had so graciously placed over me. However, I was aware of a growing restlessness in my heart. I recorded this in my journal, describing the increasing sense of God preparing Heather and me for something very different. Heather recounts how unsettling this was, as our business and home life had previously provided such security, and it seemed as if this was being eroded. In September 1995, I had to attend another gathering held in Bloemfontein, so we decided to travel back to Sunnyside in the Eastern Free State, the home of Japela and Polly. It was to be a defining moment for us. Nothing could have prepared us for what we were about to encounter.

A people waiting

We were amazed to find a vibrant Japela waiting for us on arrival. We later found out that he had been making regular enquiries with the guest farm owners as to when we would be returning, and when he heard the news of our upcoming visit, he was ready. Stepping out of the car, his first words after the traditional greetings were, "You must come; the people are waiting!"

Looking for some explanation, I asked, "Which people?"

"Everyone in the valley," Japela replied with his broad, toothy smile. To our astonishment, we discovered that since putting his faith in Jesus, Japela, with his limited understanding, had been sharing his newly acquired faith and healing with all the other villagers in the area and anyone else who would listen. And yes, they were ready! The villagers were informed that we were on our way, and they were prepared for our visit.

After deciding to meet the next day at 4 p.m., we said goodbye and settled in at the guest farm. At 4 p.m. the following day, Japela was on time and waiting for me beside our car. He directed me to a small cluster of traditional thatched huts made of daub, sticks, and clay. Entering the reed enclosure that served as a living area, what struck me immediately was the undeniable evidence of extreme poverty. An elderly couple were waiting for us. I was introduced to Japela's brother, Jacob, and his wife, Maria. I can clearly remember Jacob's home-knit jersey, with its gaping holes and loose wool threads in a dirty shade of yellow, with no shoes on his feet. Maria had come out of a very dark hut and was covered in what I later realised was soot, which made her smile appear bright. I witnessed extreme poverty among these people.

On each farm in the Eastern Free State, one found villages where the farm labourers built their own traditional houses. The basic infrastructure suggested that these dear people had no rights or support, except for the meagre earnings from local employers. The homes had no running water or provision for electricity. The women cooked over wood fires, and conditions were quite desperate, with whole families sharing a single room. The village usually had a small vegetable garden protected by an informal stick fence to keep the chickens and cattle out. If the villagers were more fortunate, they might have owned a few cattle, their only form of wealth. Clothing was scarce and made up of hand-me-downs. However, despite extreme poverty, I was to learn that these were very special people, and they were individuals from whom one could learn a great deal.

Now you must tell them!

I was pointed towards an upturned log for a seat in Jacob and Maria's little reed enclosure, and asked to join them in the tiny circle. With a white man arriving to visit, it wasn't long before the little enclosure filled up with curious onlookers from the adjoining huts. Once settled, Japela instructed me, "Now you must tell them!" If ever I had felt unprepared and incapable, it was that moment. However, Jesus gave us the promise that "the Holy Spirit will teach you . . . what you ought to say" (Luke 12:12 ESV). That was in the context of Jesus' disciples being brought before the rulers, but as I was to discover, He provides for all who carry His gospel to those who have never heard.

I asked Jacob if I could use the lovely pyracantha stick he held, which he dutifully passed to me. I then read John 14:2-3, where Jesus told His disciples, "In My Father's house are many rooms" (NASB). Japela struggled to translate, and I was overjoyed when Jacob's daughter, Topsie, understood my Afrikaans and took over the translation. Japela was all smiles! Using Jacob's stick, I began to draw the "Father's house" with its many rooms on the dusty floor of the enclosure. African people love stories and illustrations, and they received my simple line drawing of heaven in the dirt with many verbal grunts and other sounds that indicated they understood me. It was an extremely precious moment for me. I explained how our sinfulness keeps us out of a relationship with God and then told them about the benefits of knowing Him. Explaining to them the reality of man's miserable situation was visible on all the faces in that little "*makhogweng*" (reed enclosure). They watched silently, waiting for the story to unfold. I can remember pausing, letting them wait for the story to unfold further. Then came the good news! I told them how the separation was dealt with on the cross by Jesus, and what faith in His saving power does! Joy resounded, Jacob beamed, Maria nodded quietly, and Japela was a sight of absolute elation. His smile stretched across his face from ear to ear.

Those good words

My journal records that in that dusty, dirty enclosure, Jacob, Maria, their daughter Topsie, and four others surrendered their lives to Jesus. There was great joy, and then I prayed for several people with ailments. As the late afternoon "golden hour" began to put on its beautiful display in the mountains, Japela and I made a joy-filled return down the valley to the guest farm and his home. Before leaving Jacob and Maria's house, they asked if we would return the next afternoon, and so we set a meeting time for 5 p.m. They instructed me to share this wonderful story, the *"good news for the poor"*, with them once more, as they promised to call everyone together. I smiled when they called the gospel *"those good words"*.

Those good words to the test!

Returning to Heather and the boys, I discovered a different atmosphere. Heather began to tell me that, earlier in the afternoon, she noticed a couple and their two daughters sitting crying at a table in the garden. Eventually, moved with compassion, Heather went over and introduced herself, asking if she could be of any help. The father, Keith, introduced his wife Marina, and daughters René and Elaine. With many tears, Keith explained that he had been suffering from a large cancerous tumour in his spinal column. He had had two operations over the past year, hoping to remove the tumour. Sadly, it was back with a vengeance, and the medical support team were not very encouraging about the surgery he would face in four days. They had come away as a family to spend time together, knowing that the future looked bleak. Heather comforted them and then declared, "Don't worry! My husband is busy right now praying for people in the village up the road, but we will come tonight at 8:30 p.m. and pray for your healing!" I admonished her by saying, "Please tell me you didn't promise them that?" She reminded me of all that God was doing and that it was only right to offer to pray for them. I was trapped and faithless.

Later that evening, we dutifully made our way to the little chalet where they stayed. Heather introduced me and our sister-in-law Merle, who had arrived with my brother Ian, to stay with us at the guest farm. We quietly began to pray for Keith, and, as I typically do, I placed a hand on his back to join in the prayer. In doing that, I put my hand right on top of the tumour, which felt like half a tennis ball protruding from his spine. We mustered every bit of faith, and Heather and Merle spoke of God's anointing. I felt nothing and can honestly say that I felt defeated. Earlier that day, I had found ministering to the Basotho people so easy, but this felt very different.

Keith and their family were extremely grateful, and the next day, after many tears and goodbyes, they headed off to the city of Bloemfontein, where he would undergo surgery. We still had a few days left, and we so enjoyed every minute of being there, swimming, hiking, and enjoying the excellent farm meals.

Topsie and the Basotho people

As promised, Japela and I headed to an adjoining farm called Tevrede (Contentment) at 5 p.m. that day. It was a different village, and I discovered it was the home of Topsie, Jacob, and Sarah's daughters. True to their word, a large group of Basotho people gathered to hear the "good words". I was thrilled to see that God had healed Jacob, and he was walking easily, something he had previously found difficult. I was further surprised to learn that he was previously very hard of hearing, close to deaf, and that God had healed him the evening before! He was all smiles and very vocal. My journal records how "Maria glowed", quite extraordinary. Once again, in Afrikaans, I retold the story of the prodigal son and how his loving father welcomed him back. Sometimes, I wondered if I was communicating adequately, but the response was instant, and we led seven adults to Christ. Once again, there was an atmosphere of great joy. I then prayed for several people for healing, never fully understanding what was wrong with them, except that they would point to the area of their body that needed healing. They received with such faith, and many spoke of instant change, smiling and clapping with excitement. I recall being handed a newborn baby. I asked who the mother was, only to be told she was too scared of this tall white man and didn't want to come to Topsie's house. I prayed for this dear little child in the absence of its mother.

Discovering the "Daisies"

That visit to Sunnyside allowed us to make one more visit to Topsie's home the following night. But before then, we had another defining moment. Over the past few days, Heather and I had a growing sense that God was doing something in our hearts, and we began to sense that perhaps God was placing these dear people in our lives. Late into the night, we spoke through all that had happened and considered the prophetic word about "being sent to the daisies of Africa". Could they be the "daisies" that God had promised? Is this where God wanted us? As we dreamed together, we also considered all it would mean practically and all we would have to lay down in Cape Town. It felt too extreme to consider in many ways, yet there was also an undeniable measure of excitement. We laughed, sighed, and fretted, experiencing a mix of emotions. There were moments of great conversation, and then moments of silence when we were lost in thought, pondering what was happening. Did we have the courage? Heather also pointed out that, besides Keith, no one among our white friends showed interest in what was happening. That was a worry: how would we be received in the community?

At five o'clock the following evening, Heather, our newborn son Adam, and I went with Japela to our final gathering at Topsie's home. Everyone from the surrounding villages was there, and we sensed the growing togetherness, even though, socially and politically, we were not typically found together. Apartheid had brought about a great separation of people groups, but here we were now gathered as one! Once again, my journal records that "all those we prayed for the previous night were there". It goes on to describe how the very first person to receive Jesus that evening was the little sick newborn baby's mother! We found out that the child had suffered from severe colic since birth, was unable to feed normally, was continually ill, and was extremely fussy. After prayer, the child returned to her anxiously waiting mother. The baby fed normally and slept peacefully, and the mother was overwhelmed by what had happened, as there was no sign of illness. She received Jesus without hesitation. Another four also responded to the simple message that night. God was on the move. We had brought hope to the hopeless, and even though Heather and I felt vulnerable in the present uncertainty, we were rewarded by all that we saw happening around us. There were great hugs, sad goodbyes in the village, and promises of "We'll be back!" Our final goodbye was to Jacob and Maria, who we would never meet again, as they passed on shortly after our visit. And then it was a heart-warming and emotional goodbye to Japela. He was so grateful and said we must come again soon. We would have been quite amazed, as none of us knew that it would only be several weeks before we would be together again at Sunnyside. Life was about to change.

The miracle and the calling

Here is one last story before I draw this chapter to a close. The following day, we set off before dawn on our long, fourteen-hour journey to Cape Town. As always, the guest farm owner, Ann Boland, supplied us with excellent beef-and-piccalilli sandwiches for the journey. As we drove out of the farm, we passed the place where God had spoken the year before about taking the gospel to Japela. We passed Jacob and Maria's little village, with smoke lazily rising from the simple metal chimney of their hut, and finally, past the entrance to Tevrede farm, which had been the scene of so much physical and spiritual healing over the past week.

Heather and I knew that the long road ahead would allow us to consider God's call to the "daisies of Africa".

We left just before daybreak, and the sun soon rose across the vast open plains of the Free State farmlands. We were abruptly interrupted by the buzzing of my newest electronic device, a cell phone. It hardly ever made a noise because so few people had them in 1995. Heather answered it and found that it was my sister-in-law, Merle. I couldn't hear the conversation, except for Heather repeatedly saying, "Yes, we'll do that." When she concluded the call, she excitedly said, "Pull over somewhere safe; you need to call Keith Adams about his operation earlier today. He's been trying desperately to call us!" Once we found a safe place to stop and received a reasonable mobile phone signal, I called Keith on the number provided by Merle.

Keith greeted me warmly and didn't waste any time, as he had been waiting for my call. Phones did not have "speaker phone mode" in those days, so Heather ensured I repeated everything he said. His story went something like this:

> "Steve, I was not allowed to eat as usual last night because I was admitted to the Universitas Surgical Hospital in Bloemfontein early this morning. Almost immediately, the surgical team, led by my oncologist, arrived. They asked me to strip down to my underwear and to sit on one of those stainless-steel tables. They were all very kind but also quite realistic about the enormity of the task ahead of them. My oncologist then asked me to bend as far forward as possible so my spine would be fully extended in this curved position. They asked me to sit as still as possible

so that they could mark my skin as to where they needed to operate.

"As I sat still, the room went quiet, and the team of five stood behind me. I felt a few prods and could feel the oncologist pressing on the area where the tumour was. The still silence continued. Steve, the next thing I knew, was the oncologist standing in front of me and lifting my chin so he could look into my face! He then exclaimed, 'Keith, what has happened to you? The tumour has completely gone! All that we can see are the scars from the last operation! What has happened?' God has healed me!"

Keith went on to tell us how he was sent home healed. He laughed as he said he walked out with his new toiletries and toothbrush that his wife had bought the day before. As Heather and I sat on the side of the national highway in the Free State, we were overwhelmed by all God was doing. Heather and I had been worried that we had only seen God work among one people group, the Basotho. But God has shown His incredible power and love for this dear family from Bloemfontein, who represented a very different people group.

We returned to the national road, knowing God was calling us to the Eastern Free State and the 'Daisies of Africa'.

Chapter 10

IT IS TIME!

It has been said that everyone handles change differently, which is true for Heather and me. Our recently appointed South African President, Nelson Mandela, said that "to change others, you have to change yourself", and we certainly had to make enormous changes to our way of thinking. The excitement of following God's call, our recent experiences in the villages of the Eastern Free State, and all that the future now promised dominated my thinking, especially the time frame I had in mind to embark on this great adventure, and I was ready to go. For Heather, on the other hand, now a mother of three, coming to terms with all the practicalities was by far the more significant challenge, and she was processing things in a very different way. However, even with all the decisions to be made and the uncertainty about the future, we were sure that God had called us to leave Cape Town and establish a work among the Basotho people of the Eastern Free State, fourteen hours away from our current home and comfortable surroundings in Constantia Hills.

We are moving!

No sooner had we returned home from Clarens, unpacked, and settled down than we contacted Jeff and Viv Kidwell and asked if we could spend time with them the very next day. When I look back at our time together at their home, I must say that I blush at my insensitivity and lack of thoughtfulness in my timing. I began the conversation by saying, "We're moving to the Eastern Free State to plant a church!" The look on their faces said it all, and now, having led churches for many years, I smile when others gush with enthusiasm about their plans for an upcoming move, remembering this day so long ago. Over the past few years, Jeff, Viv, Heather, and I have become very dear friends, sharing many wonderful experiences. It felt as if God had moulded this friendship, and there was a deep ownership of one another, something we all appreciated and treasured.

Furthermore, Jeff trained me to become an elder, and I was now an integral part of the leadership team at The Bay. Now we were leaving! Despite my foolishness, Jeff and Viv could see that God was doing something unique and rightly encouraged us to follow a well-thought-through process of confirmation and transition. It was a happy-sad moment for the four of us. So, together, we worked out how to handle this significant change and embraced God's call.

I am grateful for the journals I have kept over the past thirty years, which record the astonishing speed at which things unfolded for us during these days. God was moving powerfully in His church; we were enjoying such times of refreshing. Our news was received with great excitement, and quickly, prophetic and Scripture-based confirmation flowed in unison with our thinking. Our boys were of the age that, if Mom and Dad were happy, they would excitedly follow and could not wait for this new adventure. However, my journal also records how Heather clarified that she was not ready or willing to consider a quick move. I recorded my frustration in my journal and withdrew to my study one night to "complain to God". How foolish I can be at times. Thankfully, God spoke clearly in that prayer time and told me, "It will be time when Heather says it is time!" That settled me, and I gave myself to our business, dreaming of the future and the very dynamic nature of church life.

It's time!

On 5th October 1995, my phone rang in my office, and my secretary announced it was Heather. At first, I couldn't understand what on earth she was trying to communicate when she said, "It is time." I tried my best to recall any commitment I had made and was now running late, but nothing came to mind. Again, "It is time." I finally asked for more information, and she said, "This is no longer home; it's time to move to the Eastern Free State."

"It is time," just like God has said. I rushed home, and for the next twenty-four hours we chatted and chatted, slowly working out the details.

Reality check

We had been praying through many things over the few weeks since our return from the Free State, and one of them was a very substantial prayer regarding our home in Constantia Hills, Cape Town. It was a simple home, but it was one we loved. One evening, God spoke to me again regarding our home and said, "You must sell the house; you are never coming back again." And so, together, after much discussion, we decided to place our home up for sale. That was a journey, but God often uses trials and perseverance to mature us. There were offers made and offers withdrawn, which sometimes left us confused and disappointed. However, times like that also reveal the kindness and love of God, and they play a significant role in developing us and teaching us to rely on Him. Sadly, none of us like facing trials or hardship, and only later can we join Paul and "rejoice in our sufferings" when experiencing His goodness. One evening, after the boys were in bed and fast asleep, I spent time before God in my study. Honestly, I was worried about Heather and the enormous cost she would incur as we settled upcountry in the central highlands. In our discussion, we considered withdrawing our boys' names from an excellent local school that was preparing to receive them. Heather had been extremely diligent from a very early stage and had registered them in this highly sought-after school; now, she would need to ask for their names to be taken off the registration list.

Furthermore, Heather has always been a great homemaker. She quickly decorated each home, and our family always enjoyed Heather's ability to make a "house a home". Now, we needed to let it go.

That evening, I sat before God with the weight of all these decisions resting heavily upon me as husband and father. As I placed these issues before God in prayer, I felt God speak again. "Go ask Heather to describe the house she will live in." God spoke about the home we still needed to find in the Eastern Free State town of Clarens, a journey we hadn't even started. But I sensed what I felt God told me to do. By this time, I had grown in discerning God's promptings.

Even so, I was extremely hesitant, knowing what serious challenges this would bring if I had misheard God. I prayed some more and, feeling a little more confident, took my journal and went to Heather, who was relaxing on the sofa in the living room, watching the evening news. As confidently as possible, I asked if I could switch off the TV and share something with her, which I did. When I told her what I believed God had said, she sat up excitedly and said, "Ooh! I like that!" I felt my confidence wane.

What kind of house would you like, Heather?

My journal describes eleven "Heather-requests". Taking the journal and pen from me, Heather wrote, "Our new home" on the open page before her. Then she made her list (written here is precisely as she wrote in my journal that evening):

Character and cosy
Possibly stone and thatch!
Big stoep [Afrikaans for veranda] with a view for chewing the cud
Comfortable bedrooms with views
Guest room
Big, eat-in kitchen (pantry)
Child-friendly and easy-to-clean
Practical and serviceable
Shower! (2 bathrooms)
Lovely child-friendly garden with space for flowers and a veggie patch
A husband to call on to make it Heather-friendly

With each line, she added a weird voice as if I were a restaurant waiter taking her order, and I felt my faith leak even further. At one point, she was about to write a request for a "master bedroom with en-suite bathroom", but I quickly pointed out that "old Free State houses don't have those", but God heard. I retrieved my journal and asked her, "When do you want it?" Heather was having fun and making the most of the situation, as her husband was obviously backed into a corner! I had hoped she would relent and say, "In two years or so?" but that was not to be. "I'm a mother, and so, like a baby, I think nine months." I retreated into my study with much to pray about; in fact, a list of eleven precise requests in nine months.

Nine months later, we moved into "Heather's new home" in the Eastern Free State, and all eleven requests were met, just like she had asked. It was a faith-builder; we celebrated God and his faithfulness and kindness, but that's for another chapter.

Where's Clarens?

Having laid everything before Jeff, Viv, and The Bay leadership team, we decided to use the church's second birthday celebration to announce that Heather, the boys, and I would be moving to plant a church in the Clarens area. On that Sunday morning, I shared the story of all God had been doing, and the energy in the room was fantastic. However, the most common response was, "Where's Clarens?" Many in our nation were unfamiliar with the small town of Clarens, especially Cape Townians, who rarely considered the Free State province except as a place to pass through on the way to Johannesburg. Yet, there was faith in the room, and we received the most encouraging response from the entire church. Someone shouted, "We're all going to plant!" bringing a great cheer from the congregation. Jeff also announced that he, Viv, and a small group from the church would accompany us to Clarens the following month to seek God and confirm our call for this move. Momentum was building, and there was great excitement, along with many emotional ups and downs, as one can imagine.

The Bay Team in Clarens

Oak Lodge is one of many chalets at the Sunnyside Guest Farm near Clarens. It is called Oak Lodge, as it is ideally positioned beneath the great-reaching branches of an ancient oak tree. In the summer, the generous oak tree keeps the two-roomed cottage cool, and it was our favourite place to stay as a family when visiting this special place. With the sandstone mountains towering over the farm, it has a majestic feel.

It was in one of the rooms in Oak Lodge that the team gathered once everyone had found their rooms and stored their belongings. The room was not large enough to accommodate a sitting area, so some of us sat on the bed, others on the two provided chairs, and the remainder of our small team sat on the floor. There was great expectancy in the room, and Jeff helpfully drew us to the focus of why we were there – had the Oliver family truly heard God? It was now late afternoon, and if you are familiar with the Eastern Free State in the summer months, you will know that this is the season for thunderstorms. These storms can be very violent at times. As Jeff prayed the very first line of his prayer, there was an air-shattering lightning strike right over our cottage! With screams from some of the team, the shockwave hit us and we were severely shaken. The thunderclap quickly followed the lightning strike, and many covered their ears as the booming effect rattled the windows as it echoed down the valley and off the cliffs above us. As the sound receded, there was much laughter, relief, and some heavy breathing; we then returned to prayer. It was a defining moment, and God had our attention.

For the next two hours, we stepped into what felt like the very presence of God, and He began to bring clarity, confirmation, and insight, leaving no doubt about our calling to move to the area and plant a church. For all of us gathered in that small room, it was like witnessing a master artist at work as he fills a blank canvas. With great care, God began to outline what our work in Clarens would entail. It started with a prophetic word: "The storm that I sent was a prophetic sign – like the storm, the church will have phases that will continue to increase and have impact." Peter Bonney, whom you may recall standing in the prayer line at our church a few weeks before travelling with us, prophesied the most shaping word, which has underpinned all we have longed for over the years. The Eastern Free State is situated on the northern side of the Drakensberg and Maluti Mountain ranges, which cross between our nation of South Africa and the Kingdom of Lesotho. With the majestic Maluti Mountains covering approximately seventy-five per cent of the nation's landmass, Lesotho is known as the Mountain Kingdom. High up in the mountains is one of Africa's great dams, the Katse Dam, which provides water for the Vaal-triangle around Johannesburg to the north. Amazingly, the

Katse Dam was commissioned the same year we planted our church. As Peter began to prophesy, he referenced the Katse Dam and said:

> "This area is the source of South Africa's three major rivers, and like the Katse Dam, God will store up His Spirit, and it will flow to all parts of our country and into the nations."

God had spoken through Pete, and our hearts resonated with what had been brought. Even though we were in one of the remotest parts of our nation, among one of the most disenfranchised people groups, seemingly unimportant to one and all, God was going to do a work in Clarens that would have international reach and impact. Right then and there, God settled something in my heart that has not left me to this day – that this was to be a work for the ends of the earth, and to all the villages, towns, and cities in between. God would use the simple things of the Eastern Free State to confound the wise. All I had ever dreamed the church could be was being detailed for us, and it was intoxicating to be so overwhelmed by God's words.

Prophetic encouragement continued to flow that afternoon, promising that God was laying down a pattern for the church, not one of human ingenuity, but Spirit-led, with signs and wonders following. It would start small in the villages and move to the ends of the earth. After a deeply impactful prayer time, we were all settled. The Olivers would be leaving Cape Town and moving to the Eastern Free State to plant a church.

Sunnyside Guest Farm is renowned for serving the most wonderful meals in the old farmhouse dining area, where large tables allow family groups to sit together and enjoy simple yet hearty meals. Small traditions at Sunnyside make it a truly special place. Individual cloth napkins with your personalised identification cloth envelope, old silverware, and the friendliest Basotho ladies, who served the meals with great skill. The dining room's flooring was comprised of timeworn oak floor planks that creaked and moaned with each step, adding to the delightful atmosphere. The flooring would have been used as ballast on ships travelling from Europe to South Africa through the treacherous southern seas, and now, for many years, it has provided flooring for the frontier houses. Course after course made the mealtime a rich event, and our Cape Town team made the most of it. The evening meal was filled with laughter and gratitude, and no one could forget the thunderclap that had occurred a few hours earlier, which resulted in continuous laughter as each person was blamed for the screams. But there was also a sense of journeying with God and a realisation that He was scattering us after a very short time together at The Bay Community Church. Heather and I had much to process, and we were grateful for the early nights enjoyed in these country areas.

The following day, we took the visiting team up to Tevrede Farm, where Topsie and many villagers had gathered among the cluster of houses. Japela was faithfully guiding us and was thoroughly enjoying all these new friends from God's family visiting his family and friends. He was full of joy and shared this most wonderful reflection with me that evening in Afrikaans: *"Ntate Steve, ek was plat, toe het die Here my opgetel."* Translated, it means, "Father Steve, I was so low but the Lord has lifted me up," which is such an example of Psalm 113:7, "He lifts the needy from the ash heap; seats them with princes" (NIV).

It was a beautiful evening, and Jeff led worship on a borrowed guitar before bringing a short encouragement from God's Word. Such a simple setting. Seven little houses of traditional daub and thatch. Chickens clucking away while constantly on the move in the red dust. This beautiful rural scene was filled with the aroma of willow branches smoking on the fires burning in readiness for the evening meal. This was Africa. This was rural Africa. This was where God wanted us. And, here we were, surrounded by "the daisies of Africa, who would reach the ends of the earth". This is what God had promised.

After four wonderful days together, the team headed back to Cape Town, while we remained in Clarens and began looking for a home in the area, which, sadly, didn't result in much success. We headed back home and started the process of planning our move.

Preparation

Shortly after my mother's death, some six years earlier, my father, Richard, joined our company in Cape Town and was the overseer of all the stock management and service teams. He was a competent, hardworking, and trustworthy person and had been a great addition to the business. Now came the hard part. Having organised some fresh tea, I called him into my office and told him the story of all we had experienced. I explained in detail all that Heather and I were carrying in our hearts and what that would mean to us. He sat quietly, listening to everything I had to share. Finally, I explained that God had called us to leave Cape Town and pursue His purposes in the Eastern Free State, and that we would be doing so through a new church plant in Clarens. My mother's untimely death had sadly hardened my father's heart towards God, and so the news of laying down so much for God and an unknown people was a bit of a shock to him. However, he reminded me of a day thirty-four years earlier when my life was almost lost during surgery because a well-meaning nurse had given me an evening meal, not realising that I was due for surgery. The complications of this nearly cost me my life. The surgeon had explained to my father that my recovery was nothing short of a miracle and that God had, indeed, a plan for this little boy's life. He had instructed my parents to ensure I was raised with a thorough knowledge of God and His purposes. So, with great tenderness, my dad released us to God's purposes, albeit with much concern for the future of the business and our boys.

For the next six months, we travelled back and forth to Clarens looking for a home. We considered old farm dwellings that had been abandoned, one or two houses in the town, but nothing matched up to the "palace" God had promised Heather a few months earlier. The fourteen-hour drive between Cape Town and Clarens was becoming a significant trial as we travelled to and fro. Finally, after months of waiting and many disappointments, our Constantia Hills home sold. It was exciting and terrifying as we still had nowhere to live in Clarens.

"This is it!"

In April 1996, tired of the many long car journeys, we decided to travel to Clarens by train, which proved to be much more complicated than it sounded. The closest station to Clarens was in Bethlehem's neighbouring market town, so we had to arrange with friends in the area to collect our well-travelled family. Our main aim for that trip was to find a home. Day after day, we combed the area with the one and only estate agent, Barbara Green. Not many people moved to this area, and there was nothing on the market. She faithfully called around, trying to find someone willing to sell their home. Our time ran out, and in the early hours of Tuesday morning, we headed to the train station feeling quite defeated. By 4 a.m., no train had arrived, so I searched for an attendant, but none could be found. I woke up a local security guard who curtly informed me that the train had left the day before and the next one was two days away! I called our friends, who faithfully returned to collect our somewhat bedraggled and irritated family. We returned to our beds at the guest farm and decided to sleep in.

Around 9 a.m. we were rudely awoken by banging on our chalet door. I sleepily opened it to find a Basotho lady telling me that there was an urgent telephone call for me in the guest house office. Making my way to the office, I picked up the landline to hear the voice of an excited Barbara Green on the other end. The estate agent said, "Can I come to collect you? I've been trying to contact you since last night! There is a beautiful farm that came onto the market last night; it's on the road towards Fouriesburg, the next town – I'll fetch you in thirty minutes!" After missing most of the previous night's sleep, I did my best to understand everything she had just said. A farm? I don't want a farm! I protested, but Barbara went on to say that there was nothing else on the market, so what did we have to lose? A few minutes later, I was persuaded and returned to the chalet to get Heather and the boys ready. As it turned out, we decided to leave the boys with carers and headed off with Barbara half an hour later.

It was a gloomy day. The cloud hung over the mountains, and there was light rain. Travelling the forty minutes to this farm, Heather and I had already decided that this would not be the place we wanted. The Maluti Mountains stood majestically in the distance as we rounded a corner at a place we now call "God's Window". The views were stunning, but we were resolute that this would not be the place. However, as we drove slowly along the gravel road that winds into the valley, something stirred in our hearts. Eventually, we turned into the long driveway, flanked by two stone pillars with wagon wheels mounted in the walls. It was here that Heather elbowed me quietly as we sat in the back seat of the car and said, "This is the place, I'm sure." I can remember looking at her with great surprise.

After the many frontier wars in these remote parts of South Africa, the government established farms along the border with the Kingdom of Lesotho. King Moshoeshoe of Lesotho was a remarkable statesman, dressed in a top hat and tails; he appealed to Queen Victoria of the British Empire for protection of his people, who were encamped at Thaba Bosiu, from the advancing Dutch settlers, known as the Boers. Queen Victoria established Lesotho as a British protectorate, and to maintain border security, the government established farms along the frontier. We arrived at Kromdraai Farm (Afrikaans for "curved road"), established in 1873. It was a common practice for the first owners of these farms to disassemble their ox wagons, and, at the right time, they would set the wheels into the gate posts as a sign of having arrived and settled. Two wagon wheels welcomed us to Kromdraai Farm.

As we parked in the wide entrance area, the old sandstone farmhouse stood before us, unloved and neglected. Passed down through numerous generations, the farm eventually went bankrupt as tensions between the farmers and local Basotho people grew. Crops would be torched, shots would be fired in anger at one another, and, generally, it was a place of great division and oppression. As we considered the history, our minds spun with the enormity of the context and all we faced. We were told that the army had used it as an outpost; two families had moved in for short periods, with one being a big game hunter, who left the antlers of a large Kudu bull mounted on the front *stoep* – it's still there today!

Heather had asked God for eleven things in her new home. Entering the house we were amazed to find that all eleven of her requests had been fulfilled. The views from the front *stoep* were breath-taking, and one could see the Rooiberge, some twenty-five miles away down the valley. What a view! The living rooms were large and airy, with beautiful bedrooms and a fabulous, if outdated, kitchen. Entering the master bedroom, I was conscious of Heather's desire to have an en-suite bathroom. Did it have an en-suite bathroom? No old Free State farmhouse had an en-suite, except this one. There it was. Heather smiled with deep satisfaction. God had given her everything. Even though the main farmhouse did not have a thatch roof, the adjoining cottage did. For us, the main house was a palace, and the next day, once again, seeing the hand of God, we signed up for the property – 610 hectares of farmland.

We had a home that required lots of work, but it was still a home. We showed our young boys the farm, and then, excitedly, we managed to catch the train and head for Cape Town. It was time to pack.

Chapter 11

HEADING NORTH TO CLARENS

The moving date was set. Heather, Cameron, Richard, Adam, two cats, a Labrador named Reg, and I would be setting off on 11th July 1996, three days after Heather's birthday. In the build-up to our departure from Cape Town, I had numerous meetings with the team at The Bay Church and with Simon Pettit, who was now emerging as an apostolic leader for our churches in Africa. It was wonderful to feel the support and ownership of our move from everyone involved, but it was not without its struggles. Doubt and fear seemed to be constant companions, and both Heather and I vacillated between a deep call for our move to Clarens and the great regret of leaving Cape Town. By starting our company twelve years prior, we had tried to ensure that we would never have to leave Cape Town, and here we were, leaving our home, family, and friends.

Lessons and values shaped from ground zero

Now that I was entering a full-time church ministry role, Simon Pettit invited me to join the Thursday morning pastors' gathering. I was both apprehensive and excited by the invitation, and it was to be a meeting that would have a lasting impact on my leadership style. For eight years, I had sat and received ministry from the men as they led, preached, and guided us from the platform. Now I was one of them! It was extremely intimidating, but I so enjoyed the togetherness and support each expressed for our unusual move to the Free State. However, the atmosphere was not what I expected. I was not accustomed to the very open and confrontational style of the meeting, and I was most distressed by how the leaders spoke to Simon, our apostolic leader. There was a noticeable lack of unity and togetherness, which surprised me. After the meeting, I approached two leaders and quizzed them on how things transpired and why there seemed to be such a lack of unity. They shared disappointments, and it became evident that this group had numerous unmet expectations. I left that gathering with many questions, and in my heart I decided there had to be a better way to build a wider group of leaders. Indeed, we could be there *for one another's success*. Did there have to be such a competitive environment among church leaders? I had much to learn, but what I witnessed was not encouraging. However, that negative experience was the catalyst for shaping the values of our present movement of churches in a positive direction.

On Sunday, 9th June 1996, Simon gathered all the churches across the Western Cape for a Sunday evening celebration in Somerset West, an hour from Cape Town. After the worship, Heather and I were ushered to the stage with our three boys and asked to share what God had called us to do. Heather was so articulate as she shared about leaving our home and the task of raising the boys in isolation, away from our family in Cape Town. There was a sense of reality, but also a great sense of adventure before us. The few hundred people prayed for us, and we received great encouragement from many across the congregation. Nicky Welsh, who was serving Simon Pettit as his administrator, brought a very shaping word, sharing that "God has chosen you for the task, only you can do it for God – it's going to be a blessed work, more than you can ever imagine". What a promise! As we left the stage, Simon reached out and took me by the arm and said, "I feel this is going to be much bigger than we ever imagined, you know that, don't you?" With that, he prayed, "Apostolic [sent one] anointing to preach the Word, preach the Word!" With that, we were sent on our way.

Three weeks later, Simon and Lindsey Pettit joined us at The Bay Church for our final send-off. It was a remarkable morning for the church as Simon was there to send us off and introduce and ordain four elders for the church, including me. And then, we were formally released to go and plant the church in Clarens. With all the goodbyes to family and friends behind us, the day arrived, and by 4 a.m. on 12th July, we were well on our way to Clarens. Our Toyota double-cab pickup was loaded to the hilt with some belongings and all the animals. It was a slow and arduous journey, but we quickly crossed the Hottentots Holland Mountains and journeyed north to our new home and into the promises of God.

During the day, we continued to hear news of snowfall (the Southern Hemisphere experiences winter in July) in the central parts of the nation. Not fully understanding the climate of our new area, we didn't take much notice or consider how it might affect us. The boys slept most of the early morning; like us, they were quiet but excited. To help them understand the substantial change they were facing, we bought Cameron and Richard a Swiss Army knife each, complete with all the included gadgets. As they were still very young, I had filed off the sharp side of the blades, but even in that condition, the knives caught their imagination, and they felt they were prepared like great adventurers. Some fourteen hours later, we entered the Eastern Free State, and what a surprise awaited us.

White welcome

It was not a light snowfall! Over a foot of snow blanketed the entire area, marking the beginning of our adventures. The trees were covered, the fields were white, and it felt as if we were the only people on earth at times. We carefully negotiated the final gravel stretch of road that led to Kromdraai Farm. Everything looked so different from what we had seen in the summer months. At times, our pickup truck and trailer snaked perilously on the turn, leaving Heather hanging on to everything that slid around in the car. Finally, in the snow, we spotted the two wagon wheels and the entrance to our home. The drive to the house was silent as we all took in the snow-covered fields. The house was dark in the gloomy evening light, giving it a spooky feel. Having collected the keys from the previous owner on our way, we entered and were home.

We stayed together as we went from room to room, investigating each empty room in the fading light. It was freezing in the house, and we quickly realised there was no power or running water. We settled the animals as soon as possible, and as we began to work out how we would spend the night in such harsh conditions, we heard the arrival of a pickup truck. To our delight, it was Ian Boland, the son of the owners of Sunnyside Guest Farm, some forty-five minutes away. I doubt Ian will ever realise how much that meant to us and how relieved we were to see someone we knew. He told us that the snow had knocked out all the power in the area and could take days to restore it. He told us they were very worried about us staying at the farm and had prepared a small cottage for us at Sunnyside. He asked us to follow him to Sunnyside as quickly as possible before it got too dark. We fed the animals, locked them in and followed Ian out of the farm. With our heads spinning from tiredness after the very long drive and the enormity of our move, we gratefully settled into the snow-covered cottage at Sunnyside Guest Farm.

After several days of travelling between our new home and Sunnyside Guest Farm, our furniture arrived from Cape Town. Navigating the long, wet, snowy gravel road was quite an adventure for the removal company employees. Snow continued to cover most of the landscape, and they did an admirable job. When it was time to leave, they decided to wait for the early morning hours, so the road would freeze, allowing them to get through what would have otherwise been severe slushy mud.

Those first few days passed in a daze as we came to terms with our new environment, taking enormous emotional energy. There were boxes everywhere, and we still needed to settle where our various pieces of furniture would be placed. The realisation that we were now responsible for our water supply and ensuring the integrity of our electricity supply rested on us, something we'd never considered when living in a city. The quality of the gravel road was also a constant challenge as the snow started to melt, and the clay on the roads became a serious issue. The boys, however, settled very quickly as there was so much to discover around the farmyard. With the quantity of snow, they were able to build their first of many snowmen, which was such fun as we tried to find a nose, eyes, and ears in a very muddled household. Adam, our youngest, was almost eighteen months old and shed many tears as the snow was both a friend and foe – his little hands would ache with the cold, which he found hard to understand. It was a significant adjustment for Heather, and the sheer number of unopened boxes was more than she could handle at that stage. The quietness of the farm was also such a challenge after the busyness of the past few months, and I would often find her sitting quietly on the front *stoep*, staring into the distance, obviously contemplating the future in this remote environment. I felt desperately sorry for her, and finding words of comfort was hard.

Darkness

Our first few nights in our new home were very interesting! We found the nights to be extremely dark, and we were surprised to discover that there wasn't another visible light in the view from our home, having lived for many years with streetlights shining through our house. Our neighbour was two kilometres away, and we had yet to meet them. At times, the only sound one would hear at night was the cry of the silver-backed jackal on the mountainside a few hundred metres away. These eerie sounds would reverberate around the valley as one cried out and another replied in a death-curdling sound. What an adjustment from suburban life in Cape Town.

As the snow started to recede, I noticed a large black shape on the land. I investigated with the two older boys and discovered a large bull Wildebeest. Wildebeest are one of the largest and most aggressive types of antelope, often seen in pictures of mass migration. Sadly, this one had died in the snow, and we are still unsure where it came from, as most of the wild game in the area is in restricted, fenced-off areas. Our farm had a herd of about twenty Blesbok, characterised by their distinctive white blaze running down their faces and a further one on their rumps. They amused us as they snorted when we came near, and we loved the way they walked in the straightest line you could ever imagine, one after the other.

In our second week in our new home, we were overjoyed to have Jeff and Viv Kidwell visit us, even though we were far from settled. We were incredibly lonely, and we were so grateful for them making the long trip to check up on us. They were shocked at how cold it was in the house, but we had lots of fun together, even having a *braai* (barbecue) in the snow. Their visit was life-giving to us, and it was a sad moment a few days later when we had to say goodbye once again when the reality of our situation finally set in.

Snake in the drain

But, amid this significant change, there were wonderful moments to remember. Late one evening, as Heather was preparing our evening meal, Richard came running into the kitchen, flapping his arms like a little bird. In his excitement, this little five-year-old couldn't quite get the words out, but eventually shouted, "Snake!" That caught our attention, as we were well aware that the farm had a variety of deadly snakes, and we had prepared the boys as best we could. After settling him down, we discovered the incredible story. Like most boys his age, Richard had gone to the bathroom to drink water straight out of the tap as getting a glass was far too much of a hassle for a farm boy. As he stuck his head into the basin to drink from the running tap, a snake had risen from the plughole right next to his face! At first, we thought it improbable, but he was sure about what he had seen. The family headed to the bathroom, slowly devising a plan where I would slide along the floor just below the height of the bathroom basin. Heather, a very animated Richard, Cameron, and little Adam would watch from the passage to see if the snake arose from the plug hole. It did!

Heather described it to me as I was below the sink; surprisingly, Richard had identified it before anyone could. We bought each of the boys a snake book as part of the new adventure, and they spent many hours studying the various snakes, especially those reported to have been found in our area. "It's a Red-Lipped Herald!" he shouted. You can imagine my next question: "Is it venomous?" I asked, and confidently, they all reported that it only gave you a severe headache but would not kill you. Great.

With Heather and the boys guiding me, we waited until enough of the snake protruded from the plughole, and I was told, "Grab it!" To my surprise, I caught it on the first go! But there was a problem. As I tried to slide the snake out of the plughole, it got stuck in the lovely brass grate! With careful manoeuvring, we discovered that it must have eaten a frog and had this enormous bulge right in the middle, which did not allow it to be removed. With me holding it tightly below the head, we had to devise another plan, which turned out to be snake-friendly, not plughole-friendly. The boys fetched some tools, and, with my free hand, I slowly prized open the plug grate until the little, Red-Lipped Herald began to emerge. When it was finally out, it was about thirty-centimetres long and had beautifully coloured markings and the most lady-like red lips. Our little adventurous family excitedly released the pipette-shaped snake in the rocks behind the house. Dinner time was filled with very engaging stories. As you can imagine, the excited little boys occasionally embellished their accounts. Richard was a star, Dad was a hero, and the plug would remain part broken for thirteen years. It was not our last snake experience, but one of many.

Adjustments

When moving to Kromdraai Farm, I had promised Heather that I would be entirely focused on her and the home for the first three months, and church work would follow. And so, slowly but surely, the house started to take shape. In moments of loneliness, my journal records the inspiration we received from God's Word, and we did our best to keep God's promises before us, even though the future seemed very uncertain. My journal also records the constant way God came through for us and how we saw His grace at work.

We were taken aback when two Basotho ladies entered our home one day. With no introduction, one declared, "I iron, she cleans." We were on the back foot and didn't know what to say. We had no plans to seek help at home as we were on a tight budget. But then came the realisation

– these dear people come with the farm – although they were free to leave and start a new life, they'd been so marginalised that they felt beholden to the farm! Their livelihood depends entirely on us! The situation was further challenging as we didn't understand each other's languages. It was an unbelievable moment when we first faced the extreme challenges of the context in which we now lived. In our moment of indecision, we let it go and slowly got to know Julia and Alina. Julia moved away shortly thereafter, but Mme Alina (Mother Alina) is still part of our family thirty years later. From this early stage, we understood that creating employment would have to become one of our highest priorities; the local people were in a desperate situation.

New experiences of farm life filled the first three months with many surprises: frozen pipes, astonishing veld fires, rats in the roof and too many stories for one book. Slowly but surely, we began to enjoy the beauty of our surroundings and found it challenging to fill the void left by family and friends. Heather had to work through tremendous pain relating to being so far from her family in those days; the cost was very real. Gratefully, we met some fellow leaders from a church two hours away, and we could travel to them on Sundays and enjoy frequent fellowship. Now and again, friends would stop over on their way up the country, which was both a blessing and a struggle, as goodbyes were especially painful. My journals record the highs and lows of these early days; we were learning that pioneering was not for the faint-hearted.

Chapter 12

FINDING A NAME – DIHLABENG

It was our first spring in the Eastern Free State, and we were amazed at how quickly the farm landscape began to change. We had only seen the dry, parchment-like grasslands, hard ground, and barren trees for our first three months, but now it seemed to burst into life! The transformation was quite exceptional! First came the richly coloured pink blossoms of all the peach trees scattered around the farm, followed by the refreshingly green leaves of the willow trees, coming to life in the valley. It was beautiful. Gone were the frosty mornings and the bleak landscape, and the cacophony of bird sounds in the morning was a pleasant surprise as they welcomed the spring. In winter, the area has a variety of shades of beige, but now, we can see a colour that is very helpful for our overall well-being. Heather was missing family and friends, and Cape Town was like the landscape; it had been a barren few months, with severe loneliness and feelings of isolation. The spring brought some much-needed relief. It was shortly followed by the spring rains, which released the most wonderful aroma from the hard-baked soil. Nothing quite like the African landscape after a shower of rain.

Small beginnings

With our family now settled into life on the farm, I began visiting those we had gathered in the Sunnyside Valley before moving to Clarens. I had regularly visited Japela and was delighted to find that they had started a Sunday gathering in the village at Sunnyside Guest Farm, led by the farm chef, Joel. In the middle of the village, a small building had been renovated to provide a space for a small group of believers. At the start of September and the coming of spring, I started joining them on Sundays, which was an absolute joy as they made me feel so welcome. Two new young ladies, Ntswaki and Mapopina, had joined the growing group and their worship leadership was stunning. There was one amusing factor about the gathering. It was an informal building, and the ceiling beams were very low. My 1.84m height proved to be an issue numerous times, and I kept hitting my head. Lifting my hands to worship was also a real challenge, and everyone started to notice, and many apologised. Solution: they removed the joining beams when I arrived for next week's meeting. I will never know how the roof stayed on, but it did solve my height issue. Although a little formal, I loved the songs sung in both Sesotho and IsiZulu and enjoyed bringing the message most Sundays. The Bible often speaks of small beginnings – indeed, this was one of them. Like the tiny mustard seed Jesus spoke about in the parables, this all felt insignificant and minuscule. Would this amount to anything?

We were delighted to be invited to a gathering of the growing number of churches looking to Simon Pettit, which was taking place in September on the southern KwaZulu-Natal coast. To be with friends from across South Africa was so refreshing for Heather and me, and our boys were delighted to find a few friends of their own. Simon's broad vision was developing, and our church leaders were encouraged to start adjusting from being mainly pastorally focused to become more mission-focused. His explanation was riveting, and we were given both practical input and encouraged to dream of what we could build together. It was a breath of fresh air spiritually for Heather and me, but quite challenging at times due to the very limiting context we were in as we were still a few months away from seeing anything on the ground.

A ray of sunshine!

Enter Ray Lowe. Simon was delighted to introduce Ray and Sue Lowe, who were experienced church leaders, and Ray had a substantial international ministry. From the moment he began to minister, Ray, who is small in stature, lifted our heads and expectations with his clear Bible teaching and inspiring stories. His evident love and pride for his local church in Biggin Hill, Kent, England, was infectious. I remember thinking, "Dynamite sure comes in small packages!" and Ray was dynamite. It was also the first of many times I would hear Ray teach on Acts 11, where the Jerusalem apostles sent a humble servant leader, Barnabas, to investigate what was happening in the new church plant in Antioch, Syria. It was a breath-taking message for me and became one that has profoundly shaped my thinking over the years. Ray emphasised the statement, "Barnabas saw the grace of God", and then asked us, "What exactly did Barnabas see? What does the grace of God look like in a local church?" Even after all these years, I can clearly remember the points of that message, as they have become so foundational for me. Ray expressed that one would find liberty, generosity, genuine relationships, grateful people, joy, humility, and signs and wonders in the church. Simon Pettit, Ray Lowe, and others served us so well, and it was such a superb time of encouragement for Heather and me in those early days.

Then, a strange thing happened. As the weekend drew to a close and we prepared for our return to the farm, Ray Lowe approached me. "I've been looking for you!" I was taken aback, but he explained that he had heard of our call "to the daisies of Africa" and wanted to visit Heather and me on the farm. Tentatively, I explained that we didn't have anything on the ground yet and only planned to plant the church in November. Ray shared how God encouraged him to seek us out and spend time with us. We felt immensely honoured, and arrangements were confirmed.

It's a four-hour drive from the coast of KwaZulu-Natal back to Clarens. The route takes one through the northern Drakensberg Mountains, which are extremely beautiful. The rolling hills dotted with small *rondavol* homesteads, herds of cattle, and the greenest of pastures make for the most exquisite scenery, explaining why it was declared a World Heritage Site. But as you begin the rise to the "highveld", one can glimpse the Amphitheatre, a large mountainous area that rises well over three thousand metres above sea level. Once on the escarpment, you wind your way through Phuthaditjhaba, and you are then greeted by the majestic Golden Gate, which is part of the Northern Drakensberg and Rooiberge ranges. Even with the natural beauty of our surroundings, we couldn't hide the loneliness that greeted us as we entered our farm. After four days with all our friends, it was back to the remoteness of the life God had called us to. We were highly grateful for Ray and Sue Lowe's visit a few days later.

Adjacent to our farmhouse is a small rustic cottage, and on their arrival at Kromdraai, we decided that was where we would accommodate Ray and Sue, even though we hadn't used it very much. This turned out to be a bit of a challenge when the toilet system misbehaved. Much to my surprise, I found Ray in yellow kitchen gloves and a stick, busily unblocking the pipes. It was very embarrassing as I knew he was one of the senior members of the team who oversaw our church movement. He remained unperturbed and managed to resolve the problem. Having sat and listened to Ray minister the entire weekend, I was pretty amazed at how relaxed and accessible he and Sue were. So often, those with a high public profile keep themselves at a distance, but this was not the case with Ray and Sue, or other Newfrontiers leaders we would meet over the years. Our dinner-time conversation was filled with laughter, questions, and stories, and they were very down-to-earth. We were not allowed to keep even the smallest detail of our journey to ourselves; they wanted to know every little element of how we came to be in Clarens.

I can see it!

The next day, Ray suggested that he and I get some time together, which we did by finding a quiet place on the front lawn in the sun. I was intrigued by this man, his presence, and his genuine interest in everything about us. Then Ray asked, "Tell me what God has placed in your heart." At no time before, even though I carried many deep thoughts, had I ever revealed what God had called us to do in any great detail. It was mainly because everything sounded too flamboyant and possibly even unbelievable, given that we had not established anything yet. Taking a deep breath, I shared the vision God had given us. I explained how I longed to see a community of the Spirit, a healthy church established from among the poor, the local Basotho people, whom God would raise, and then, beginning locally, send out worldwide, establishing churches and other ministries. I shared how I longed for a radical response from these people to the love of God, which would result in a sacrificial lifestyle and the birth of many churches. With each word, my passion began to grow, and I was thrilled to be able to share my innermost thoughts so freely about my call. It would have been difficult for many to have faith in this early stage, but I was delighted when Ray said, "I can see it!" A togetherness was born in our hearts that day, as we believed in what God had promised. Our togetherness continues to this day.

Homeschooling

With just a few weeks to go before we planted the church, Heather and I set about finishing our home as best as possible. At this time, Heather began the early stages of our schooling programme for the boys. Before leaving Cape Town, Heather had felt quite stirred by the benefits of homeschooling our children. Visiting various people who had schooled their children in this manner, she gained valuable insight, and although there were drawbacks, she was convinced that it would be in the best interests of our boys, and I gave her my full support. She would gather the two older ones and begin their education each day. The wonderful thing about this form of schooling is that one's lifestyle adjusts so that every opportunity is a lesson.

But there were also scary moments for us on the farm. Behind our kitchen area, the ground rises to protect the house against the cold winter wind from the south. It's very well positioned and includes some beautiful sandstone rocks and indigenous trees. The boys loved this area and spent many hours playing among the rocks. One morning, Richard appeared at the back door, having been sent by Cameron to ask for help. "We're trying to play our game, but a snake keeps getting in the way." Heather yelled for me, and we rushed to the rocks to see what was happening. There, on a large flat area where the boys had set up camp, lay the largest puffadder one could get. This diamond-backed snake was sunning itself, and with each movement of the boys nearby, it recoiled in readiness to strike. If there is one snake to avoid, it's the puffadder. It is thick and cumbersome, getting no longer than ninety centimetres, but it has one of the fastest strikes out of all our South African snakes. Its venom is deadly and causes the deterioration of the capillaries and blood vessels.

Heather and I were shocked to find our two young boys playing so close to this deadly snake. Like a mother hen, Heather gathered her boys, who had been forbidden from playing there for many years. The snake? Well, gingerly, I manoeuvred it into a large black dustbin, which was taken two kilometres away and released. I know what you are thinking!

Church in the mountaintops!

With the excitement of farm life around us, I began to dream about what the new church would be like. I had noticed that most of the churches in the area had the most elaborate religious names, so I asked God to guide me to a fitting name. As we were high up in the mountainous regions of the nation, I began with names that reflected our locale. Finally, I settled on "Church in the Mountaintops", but it needed to be in Sesotho. It proved quite tricky, and I ended up with several variations. One afternoon, whilst visiting the Sunnyside congregation, I saw a man I had met many years ago and knew his English was good. I pulled up next to him and asked him if he could help me. It was to be the first time I would hear the word *"lihlabeng"*. In Sesotho, the "D" sound is written "Li", which I immediately recognised as a challenge for our future English-speaking members. And so, with my heart resonating with the Spirit's prompting, I knew I had discovered the church's name. Changing the "Li" to "D", I settled that the new church would be called Dihlabeng Church, or Church in the Mountaintops. Now I could genuinely dream!

Chapter 13

PREPARING TO PLANT

It was confirmed. The Bay Community Church in Cape Town, where Heather and I had begun our journey, would send ten people to join us in planting Kereke ya Dihlabeng (Church in the Mountaintops). After almost four months on the farm, it was time to plant the church. With little detail of what this would look like or how we would go about it, we welcomed our friends from Cape Town. We were also joined by a church leader from Pietermaritzburg, Craig Botha, who had tremendous cross-cultural experience. I asked him to oversee the birth of this new church and bring the main message on Sunday. I was overjoyed to hear that Peter Bonney was leading the team from Cape Town, as our friendship and companionship in the gospel were growing and growing. Sunday 3rd November was the church planting day.

Led by the prophetic

With everyone arriving on Monday for the church plant, we started by gathering in the large steel barn adjacent to our home. It was filled with old farm equipment, hay, and even an old tractor. We made a small space among all the implements and gave ourselves to prayer on Tuesday morning. Very quickly, one could sense the deep presence of God among us, and heavenly instruction started to flow. From the outset, it was clear that God was with us and we all sensed it, feeling a deep sense of excitement. There were two very instructive and clear prophetic words:

> *"I see a large wagon wheel, not dissimilar to those in the front gate post of the farm. I see the church plant like the hub at the centre of the wagon wheel, and I can see people walking, riding, and travelling in from every direction to the church gathering on Sunday, just like the spokes of the wheel. From the north, the south, east, and the west, people are coming, as if sent by God."*

It was a vivid picture, and as we gazed out of the large barn doors across the vacant lands, one could imagine the sight of people making their way towards us. At that moment, there wasn't a person in sight, but we were very excited at the prospect. We had no idea where they would come from, but God had given us very clear insight into His plans.

And then secondly:

> *"Prepare for five hundred people on Sunday."*

The first word resonated in our hearts; we all saw and believed it. However, the second prophetic word changed everything! Five hundred people, here? In these remote surroundings? It was difficult to imagine how five hundred individuals would attend the church plant meeting, where our nearest neighbour was two kilometres away. I instructed everyone to stand in a circle, look outwards, picturing the wagon wheel, and then head across the farm and "call in those God had promised to send". Faithfully, each team member headed out in their allotted direction and prayed fervently for the fulfilment of God's word. When we returned, great excitement and much debate followed about the promise of five hundred joining us on Sunday. Was God saying it would be a large crowd, or were literally five hundred coming on Sunday? Additionally, we weren't sure where to meet, as the large crowd would require a spacious venue. With much laughter, prayer, and togetherness, we decided to trust God and prepare for five hundred attendees. Why not believe God? Then, someone suggested we use the large barn where we met. It had enough space and could easily seat more than five hundred. We had five days to go. We realised that it would take a mammoth effort to clear such a chaotic steel shed quickly, but we set about our task.

Preparing for five hundred

Each evening of the week, we travelled to a different location in the area, sang a few songs and then informed everyone of the meeting on Sunday. Most people were inquisitive and welcoming. It was hard to gauge if they would arrive or not. We quickly realised that transport was going to be an issue and made enquiries. To our delight, we found a man named Solomon who had a forty-seater bus and agreed to collect those waiting along the road from as far as Golden Gate, some forty-five kilometres away. The week was taking shape.

We continued to work in the large steel shed each day and were amazed at some of the things we found, including old stoves, tractor parts, and numerous old farm tools and furniture. When moving all the loose hay, we found a puffadder hiding in the corner and were grateful to get him out of there. Slowly but surely, the barn took shape. Helpfully, there were over a hundred and fifty square hay bales, and we positioned them to create seating for five hundred people.

A team of four brought some cloths and painted a few banners to brighten up the rather dark and gloomy room. One victoriously proclaimed, "Ever-increasing Glory", the promise of 2 Corinthians 3:18, which speaks of the transformational work of Jesus in our hearts. Another group headed to the nearest town of Bethlehem and purchased supplies that would enable us to provide each of the five hundred people with a small, simple meal after the meeting. It was a mountain of potatoes, rolls, apples, paper plates, juice and five hundred sausages. Quietly, everyone hoped five hundred people would arrive, or a lot of food would be left over.

In situations like this, finance was always a challenge. We were unsure how to arrange such a large event, but God is faithful. The week before, Ray Lowe phoned from the UK and encouraged me that he, Sue, and the church were praying for us and "owning" our vision, even though they were far away. It was lovely to hear from him again, and he then informed me that they had collected £400 for us, the exact amount we needed. It added to our faith, and we were buoyant by God's provision through our friends.

One of my special tasks of the week was travelling to Sunnyside Farm to meet Ntate Japela and inform him about all our preparations and what would take place on Sunday. He was delighted, and I told him that I would collect him on Sunday morning so that he could witness what was about to be born through our togetherness in the gospel. He was now quite frail, and sadly, Mme Polly, his wife, would not be able to join us as she too was very feeble. Ntate Japela had undoubtedly become my "man of peace", facilitating such an astonishing move of God across the area. Jesus had sent His disciples out to every town and village, instructing them to find a man of peace who would welcome them in. Ntate Japela was precisely that to me, and now we are reaping the rewards of his faithfulness. I couldn't wait for him to see what God would do, even though his understanding of the effectiveness of church planting might be limited. Together, we had found God, and together we would reap a harvest.

Having the team was such a blessing for Heather, the boys and me. The boys loved all the attention and renewed friendships, as the team gave them so much time. Each evening, we would *braai* together on the front lawn, play games, and there was lots of celebration. We were walking in faith, believing God for something "unseen", which was fabulous. One could sense that God was doing something unusual and exciting in the simplicity of our surroundings. The large steel barn stood ready, banners up, hay bales neatly positioned, a simple stage erected, and the food was about ready. Now we needed God to come through for us.

Chapter 14
THE BIRTH – DIHLABENG CHURCH

Sunday church plant day arrived, clothed in magnificence! The most beautiful Free State morning greeted us with bright blue, clear skies, no clouds, but sun-kissed green fields. Early in the morning, I found a quiet place to sit before God on this most important day. For me, it felt like this day would be a high point of my life and much of the reason God had called us to the Free State. As we started the day, there were still many unknowns, but I also remember having a quiet assurance that God was ever so near. Sonship is a wonderful thing, and I sensed His affirmation as a kind Father, ever-present and involved.

While praying, I felt God led me to the story in John chapter 11 of Jesus and the raising of Lazarus from the dead. Lazarus, a man from the town of Bethany just outside of Jerusalem, had become a dear friend of Jesus, but sadly, in Jesus' absence, he had taken ill, died, and was duly buried. His sisters were distraught, knowing that if Jesus had been present, Lazarus would have lived. Now, four days later, Jesus arrives in Bethany and is deeply moved to tears at the loss of this friend. The account of this story records how

Jesus gathers them at the tomb and instructs them to open it, which was met with great resistance due to the perceived state of Lazarus' body. Ultimately, family and friends roll back the stone at the tomb's entrance. Jesus called Lazarus out of the tomb, and Lazarus walked out, raised from the dead, still wrapped in his grave clothes. What a story!

Call forth the church to life!

In that moment of solitude, God spoke clearly to me and said, "Steven, speak to the tomb of the Free State, call forth Dihlabeng Church, pull off the grave clothes, bring hope, bring life, and go forth!"

The word birthed great boldness in my heart, and I could feel what we could expect to see on that memorable day in November 1996. What was dead and decaying would be brought back to life, with purpose, bringing hope and life to many. The Free State province was not a place of influence or fruitfulness in our nation; no one expected it to be a place of "life", like Nathanael's declaration, "What good can come out of Bethlehem" (see John 1:46). That verse seemed to apply to us as well. God had set out His intentions for us, and I was very grateful for God's gentleness and comfort. On this day, we will see a miracle! Only God can give life.

Everyone on the team had their tasks, resulting in a great flurry of activity on the farm. All the vehicles were dispatched to different locations to collect people as promised, and the rest were prepared for what was to be our big day. Tim Steinke, a young man from Jubilee Church, Cape Town, had travelled up to help lead the worship. From early on, one could hear him and a team member, Sheldon Kidwell, faithfully working their way through their chosen songs, including "Sing for joy oh, Africa, the Lord your God has risen upon you now!" which seemed particularly fitting. Our little Adam, almost two years old, had a small, handmade wooden guitar that I had made for him, and he joined them, happily waddling around in his nappy. Everyone had their responsibility, and no one needed to be coaxed into a task; it was incredible to witness. *"Bayete, Bayete, in Kosi!* Salute, Salute the King!" resonated out of the well-prepared shed. The makeshift stage, balancing on a few hay bales, sheets of board and a large tarpaulin covering, seemed to be holding, and the sound didn't seem as severe as we imagined it might be in such a cavernous steel structure. Earlier in the week, we had dug a deep pit *braai*, over which endless sausages would be cooked. As we lit the fires, the farmyard had a warm and inviting festive feel, and we were ready.

The people come

By 9:30 a.m., people began to arrive across the fields from all directions: individuals, pairs, and small groups. Brightly coloured clothing was visible, and some vibrant red umbrellas, meant to shield from the warm morning sun, dotted the landscape. What a sight! More people appeared over the fields, on the road, and from beyond the hills at the back of our farmstead. Dust billowed in the valley as an increasing number of vehicles approached the farmyard, each following marked tracks through the field to the large gathering shed. Near 10 a.m., we all gathered outside as Solomon's bus rounded the bend in the dirt road. It wasn't the engine's sound that caught our attention, but the singing and jubilant cheerfulness spilling from the bus's open windows! A video recorded by one of our team members on board showed how Mapopina marched up and down the aisle, loudly leading a rendition of *"Re tsemaya, Jerusalema"* ("We are going to the new Jerusalem"). Their excitement was palpable, heightening the anticipation of the entire team, who had spent the whole week with this moment in mind.

Slowly but surely, the large barn began to fill up. Each person found their place among the hay bales and sat quietly. The air was thick with anticipation. One by one, the people arrived. A noisy sound announced the arrival of a tractor and trailer loaded with people, happily hanging on for dear life. A local farmer had allowed his staff to use it to ferry people from the surrounding villages, and the tractor manoeuvred outside the barn, coming to a halt, which allowed another large group to find their way inside hastily. It was a colourful, noisy scene. The farm transformed from its usual peaceful state to a place bustling with excitement.

Ntate Japela, who had arrived earlier that morning, sat in a comfortable chair in the doorway, smartly dressed for the occasion and backlit by the bright morning outside. He looked very serene and statesman-like as he sat in his chair. Small beginnings on the mud step of his tiny home two years before were now ushering in a significant event.

Come to Jesus!

With the meeting underway, worship filled the barn, which was now packed to capacity. God had come through for us;

Japela Semaase some years before his conversion

Polly Semaase

Japela and Polly's Village at Sunnyside farm

Steve and Japela in 1996

Japela Semaase 1995
after his conversion

Recent photo of Angus Houston and Steve

Arriving at Kromdraai Farm July 1996

Homeschooling the three boys at Kromdraai Farm

Steve and Billy the Blesbok

The barn prepared for the church plant on 3rd November 1996

Dihlabeng Church 1997

Steve and Justice leading in the barn

Baptisms in the Mohokare River

Baptism joy!

Dihlabeng Church retuning from baptisms at the river

Master Builders Banner 2005

A young Fusi Mokoena preaching at Master Builders

Dihlabeng Church 2006

The original Dihlabeng team:
Steve Oliver, Justice Mofokeng, Peter Bonney and Gavin Northcote

The Oliver Family

there were hundreds in attendance. It's hard to confirm, but it must have been many years since such a large multi-cultural group had met and worshipped in this area. In our previously divided nation, this practice had been forbidden, but now, here we were, shoulder to shoulder, lifting the name of Jesus and hope. It was path-breaking but also almost too much to take in. After the welcome, Craig Botha ministered to us, clearly sharing the hope found in the gospel of Jesus Christ. The crowd were amazingly attentive even though it was very hot in the barn. Children sat quietly as the message resonated around in the large structure. The message concluded with Craig calling out, "Come to Jesus, come to Jesus!"

A church is born

Halfway back, a slightly built Basotho lady stood up and went to the front. Her boldness seemed to unlock a flood of others. I later learned that it was Mme Maria. Another two, then a few more, and so it went. Craig stirred a group of men in the room to respond to Jesus, who then walked to the front. Sixty-four stood together, surrendering and following Craig's prayer. With the acknowledgement of their sinful state and the need for Jesus' forgiveness, joy started to flow, and it was a marvellous moment. Dihlabeng Church had been born, and here it was, producing its first gospel fruit. Each one got prayed for, and there were many hugs and tears. One of my lasting memories was that of a white South African woman with her arms wrapped tightly around a black Basotho woman who had equally responded by holding tightly onto her new friend. They stood there for ages, tears flowing, as they expressed their need and appreciation for one another. Jesus ushered in a new community when He sacrificed everything on the cross, and here we were, two thousand-plus years later, seeing the fruition of that great act.

We prayed for the sick, danced, laughed, and hugged. I embraced Heather as we took in the scenes in the barn, knowing the great sacrifice that had brought us to this place. Soon, the smell of the sausages on the *braai* outside got the better of us, and we invited everyone to line up outside and collect their lunch. No second invitation was necessary, and the colourful crowd joyfully queued in the yard. It was all so easy and wonderfully ordered, and the celebration of what God had done continued among the crowd. As part of the celebration, we announced that the church would meet every Sunday at 10 a.m. This announcement was received with great excitement.

The five-hundredth!

The last people left at about 3:30 p.m.; it had been a mammoth event. The Cape Town team, as we were, was exhausted, but this did not take away our amazement at what we had experienced. We all decided to rest and then re-gather in the evening to celebrate. Heather and I were cleaning our kitchen at about 5 p.m., chatting through all we had seen and enjoyed. Laughingly, Heather pointed out that I was a false prophet, as there was one meal left, meaning that we had fed four hundred and ninety-nine people. As we laughed together, there was a loud knock on the front door, and I went to investigate. Standing on the front doorstep was an older man in white overalls, hat in hand. We greeted each other, and he asked me if he was too late for the meeting! Yes, I explained and told him all about what had happened. Saddened, he told me he had walked for many hours from the foothills of the Maluti Mountains and apologised for missing it. I suddenly recalled that we had one meal left! Smugly, I returned to the kitchen and asked Heather for the *one* remaining meal, explaining that 'number five hundred' was at the front door. I often remind her of that sweet moment and the older man at the door. Isn't God just so wonderful?

Ever-increasing glory!

Our final evening with the Cape Town team was spent discussing our wonderful week together. At times, there was an atmosphere of deep reverence as we realised we had experienced something unique. It had been God's week, His plant, His people, and He had great things in store for Dihlabeng Church. We reflected on the banner above the stage: "Ever-increasing Glory". If this was the start of what God would do, this church was in for an incredible experience.

Chapter 15

MY NAME IS JUSTICE, I'VE COME TO BE SAVED!

Church planting is not for the faint-hearted. With the backdrop of the opening celebration behind us, we prepared for our first post-plant Sunday meeting in the steel barn, and expectations were high as everything began to fall into place. My journal referenced the opening week and the extraordinary nature of that day. I recorded:

3rd November 1996

"Today we have seen Dihlabeng Church born into the Free State, SA. 500+ folk gathered to declare the birth. Sixty-two responded to the message and received new life! Thank You, Lord, for life! On this beautiful day, we have seen such great things – worship, prayer, the word, salvation, and the Holy Spirit. Dihlabeng received life."

However, the following week, the African rains began to fall on Friday, increasing on Saturday, and resulting in a very wet and muddy Sunday. By the time we were due to start our morning meeting, twelve bedraggled individuals sat quietly on the hay bales. After the highs of the previous week, this had to be the lowest I had felt for many months. It was such a let down.

However, there was one moment of joy when a small group of ladies from Lesotho arrived, led by a smiling Mme Alisia. I had heard that the Mohokare River, bordering Lesotho, was in flood and impassable, and so I was intrigued as to how they had managed to get across and reach the service. With much laughter, Mme Alisia explained how they had taken off their outer garments, each placed a bundle of clothes on their heads, and slowly swam carefully across the river, helping one another to navigate the ever-swelling river. I was amazed that Mme Alisia, who was only four-feet-six-inches tall – a truly diminutive lady – had shown such courage and determination to attend the meeting. Looking back, I can now see that this was a significant prophetic picture of the nature of the dynamic yet straightforward community of Dihlabeng.

Sunshine greeted us on our third Sunday, and I held my breath to see how the day was to unfold. It was to be a life-changing day, although my diary reflects a problematic start to the day:

16th November 1996

"Went to collect those from Golden Gate – very disappointed, only 1. Returned to the farm to find nobody. Went along our gravel road to Mooidam Farm – a handful waiting! Many trips later, 80 at the meeting. Thirty-seven adults and the rest are children. I was greatly disappointed, but I preached as best as I could. Asked those who had not responded the week

before to come forward and receive Jesus. 28 saved!!! God is wonderful.

"As I've said, church planting is not for the faint-hearted."

Just before the start of the third week at the church, I decided to walk across the wide farmyard and check in on Heather and the children as they readied themselves for the meeting. As I made my way across the sunny, dusty area, I noticed a tall young Basotho man making his way up the long driveway. His demeanour was one of stature, and so I stopped and waited for him at the top of the roadway. He was unusually tall for a Basotho man, and on approaching me, he stretched out his hand to introduce himself with one of the most impactful statements I had ever heard. "My name is Justice, I've come to be 'saved'." What a moment, what a man, what a Saviour. Justice was one of the twenty-eight who made their way to the front and surrendered to Jesus that third Sunday morning.

After the joyous time in the large steel shed, we closed the meeting, which had approximately eighty-plus adults in attendance, and sent everyone on their way. I caught Justice on his way out and asked him if he would like to stay for what was now to be a mid-afternoon lunch. Nervously, which I was later to understand, he accepted and asked if he could invite a friend, Elias, to join us. Together, we made our way into the kitchen and chatted while Heather prepared a meal. Over a simple lunch, we listened to Justice's story with utter amazement, hanging on every word as he shared why he had come to Dihlabeng Church that morning.

Growing up under Apartheid

The Free State province of South Africa represented much of the heartland of the Apartheid government that had previously ruled over our nation for some forty years before freedom. Farm labourers were some of the most abused employees in our country, more slave-like, with very few rights or opportunities. Life was hard. Justice was born to his parents, Ntate Nuwejaar (New Year) and Mme Mamotseke Mofokeng, in 1964 on the farm Heather and I had bought some thirty years later, called Kromdraai Farm. Their informal home was one of five in the farm village, situated within a barbed-wire-fenced area of approximately one acre. For Justice and his siblings, life was confined to the fenced area, and they were only allowed outside this boundary when fulfilling their farm tasks. Life was harsh, and Justice shared how his parents worked long, difficult hours on the farm. Anyone trespassing across the lands was met with gunfire over their heads from the aggressive owners, creating a tense and scary environment for any child to grow up in. From the age of fifteen, every child was expected to work on the farm, which led Justice's parents to make a huge decision.

Late one night, Justice was awakened to be told to carry his bedding, and the whole family slowly and quietly left their home, crossed the Mohokare River, and set up a new home in the neighbouring nation of Lesotho. And so, free of the ongoing oppression, Ntate Nuwejaar, Mme Mamotseke, and family settled into rural village life in Bafokeng, Lesotho, the Mountain Kingdom. These villages were composed of small family clans, comprising ten to twenty thatched *rondavel* houses. Stick-and-daub walls made beautiful little round homes while the usual sounds of chickens, cows, sheep, and goats accompanied village life. It's a peaceful lifestyle, yet tensions remained high with the neighbours across the river. At sixteen years old, Justice set his sights on his studies and the dream of becoming a police officer. This dream was cruelly interrupted in the early 1990s when gunshots were fired from across the river at some youth throwing rocks at a passing farmer driving along the riverbank below, resulting in a stray bullet hitting Justice's grandmother, Mme Malomele, killing her instantly. Hatred between those on either side of the river grew and grew.

With the backdrop of tension along the border areas, Justice applied to become a policeman. He was now twenty-six years old and stood a good chance of realising his dream. However, every time he went for the interview, they would get as far as him in the line and explain that their quota was filled, leaving Justice confused and frustrated. After experiencing this twice, hopelessness ensued. But then, an unusual recurring encounter marked the next few months in 1992 and 1993.

The man at night and the albino witch doctor

Over several months, Justice repeatedly dreamt of a kind, unusual man visiting him at night. This gentle visitor would appear in his dreams and say, "You will not find work, as I have called you to teach your people from this book." Each time, the man would show him a large, open book. Unsure how to respond or who he was, Justice would tell his mother about these encounters, and she would immediately take him to a witch doctor in a nearby village called Moteng.

Justice shared how his mother would cry upon hearing about this visitor, who had now appeared three times in the night. Crying out to the albino witch doctor named Moshapa, she explained that he was meant to be a policeman and needed to do his magic to help them. Each visit was costly for the family, but Justice's mother remained firm about the necessary course of action to ensure her son could support her. On the third visit to Moshapa, the worried witch doctor told Justice, "You mustn't come back to me, you know who you must go to. You have such 'light' in you – if I try medicine again, it will destroy me!" That marked their last visit to Moteng village and the albino witch doctor named Moshapa.

As we sat awestruck around our kitchen table listening to this intriguing story, Justice concluded the account of his life by telling us why he had come to be saved. Two weeks before the church plant on our farm, the night visitor appeared again. This time, he had a very specific message. "In two weeks, there will be a big party across the river where you were born. You must go; you will meet me there!" But, full of emotion, Justice told us that he didn't attend the launch as he was too scared to face the suffering he had experienced at our farm. We sat in silence, overwhelmed by the incredible story of God's grace.

In my little study in Constantia, Cape Town, a year before this meeting, God had promised me that He had prepared leaders for the church and that I was not to go looking for them. Now they sat here at my kitchen table, called by God, present and changed. Justice was not to be the last with an incredible God-story.

Chapter 16

RURAL REVIVAL

Bales of hay for sermon props

Justice and Elias' addition to us added significant momentum to the newly born Dihlabeng Church. It was a joy to watch the grace of God gather Justice up into His purposes and see him flourish as the weeks went on. Elias' gift on our simple keyboard, precariously balanced on two hay bales, released a fresh wave of worship among us. Week after week, the numbers grew with many saved each Sunday, and a number during the week as well. Such was the momentum that people invited friends and families. Many flocked to the vibrant Sunday meetings. Healing was a constant, as God worked signs and wonders among us. We saw the sick being carried into the meeting in blankets and even in a wheelbarrow on one occasion, only to return home with a folded blanket under their arm, completely healed. My simple preaching unlocked a people group, and it was never difficult to get an immediate response to the preached Word. One Sunday, to express the Father's heart for these beautiful people, I built the throne of God out of hay bales, putting on display the Father's accessibility, grace, and love. God responded with great favour upon us; it was a beautiful thing to see.

Heather and I were overjoyed when one of the team members who had assisted with the church plant, Keith Gough, contacted us to say that he was willing to travel to be with us and serve the church for a season. Having an extra pair of hands was such an encouragement; we were grateful for Keith's sacrifice and servanthood during those days.

Days of favour

These were exhilarating days for any church planter, and it felt as though we were experiencing revival. By the end of our first month, we had some two hundred adults attending our church service, which was both invigorating and stretching. My journal records that on 24th November 1996, sixty-eight responded to the gospel. On 1st December 1996, another forty people surrendered their lives to Christ. It goes on to record, "When we then prayed for the sick, the queue was so long!" Justice became invaluable to me as we prayed for people. He would ask what they had come forward for, and then I'd pray, simple, faith-filled prayers. These were exciting and powerful times. Meetings were long and drawn out, but one stood in awe of God as we watched Him at work.

One lady, Mme Malebaleng Lentsa accompanied by her daughter Maphaseka, walked from Lesotho and quietly asked for prayer at the end of the meeting. It was only later that we heard that she had severe heart issues and was unable to do the simplest of tasks in the home. Her other daughters were vehemently opposed to our church plant as it was led by a white South African, but woke up the following morning to hear their mother chopping wood! They rushed to her and asked what she was doing, as they scolded her for engaging in such strenuous activity. She told them that God had healed her completely the day before. With evidence of such a dramatic healing, Nini and Mafantere, her two daughters, made their way to us the following week and were wonderfully saved, both very quickly becoming integral and active members of Dihlabeng Church. The stories of God's grace through healing over this season are endless, and every week we continued to see numerous people respond to the call to salvation. These were amazing days.

Spiritual warfare

However, in the background, there were rumblings of opposition. Heather and I faced increased pressure on our family, and the constant demands of the growing church community stretched us to the limit. Every Saturday, we seemed to have untimely incidents, such was the spiritual warfare at the time. Our eldest son, Cameron, would have the most frightening dreams that would wake the entire family, and it would take a few hours to settle the boys. He had such a sensitivity to the spiritual realms, and it was distressing to witness. Eventually, we had to stop holding meetings in our home, as Cameron was so susceptible to all the demonic activity we were encountering as we discipled potential leaders. My diary records deep anguish in prayer to God for my family as they paid a heavy price. These were tough times indeed.

Furthermore, the local border authorities were finding it a real challenge that so many people were crossing the river from Lesotho to attend the meetings on Sundays. They would harass the people, and a growing sense of tension prevailed on Sundays. At first, they tolerated our togetherness, but this was soon to boil over.

Baptise the nations in My name

Each week, we could see the growing maturity expressed through our worship, relationships, and participation. I had begun to identify a group of potential leaders and devoted considerable time to developing them. The sense of God doing something very special continued week after week, and it was to culminate at the year's end, with the baptism of our first group of disciples. With detailed preparation, we set up at the river's edge, the most peaceful and serene place for our first baptism service. The Mohokare River (Caledon River) is situated a mile and a half from our home on the eastern side of our property. The day would start in the barn with worship, then we would form a large column of worshippers and make the mile journey down to the river. I was thrilled to hear that two families from The Bay Community Church in Cape Town were travelling up to join us, adding to the special nature of this fruitful event.

Sunday 22nd December 1996, turned out to be a magnificent day after some potent thunderstorms. The great big steel barn quickly filled up with the most colourful community imaginable, and it was wonderful to share the fruit of our first two months as a church with the Oosthuyzen and Bonney families from Cape Town. The lively worship was the ideal preparation for our march to the river, and it was a moment to behold – hundreds of singing, joyful, redeemed people, setting off in a long column towards the river.

Going down to the river

Arriving down at the river, we were thrilled to see many lining the banks on the Lesotho side as well, making it feel like a stadium spectacle. I preached a short gospel message, and, once again, my diary records that some thirty responded, some crossing the river from Lesotho in response to the appeal; how appropriate. Thereafter, with our worship team singing the most wonderful local song, "If people believe, then baptise them in the name of Jesus", Keith and I entered the water to gather those ready for baptism. It was so fitting – Keith and I had held this growing community together, and now we were celebrating our fruitfulness in a very real way. The photo on the front cover of this book caught that moment as ninety-two formed a long colourful "snake of people", curving down the banks of the Mohokare River and into the waters of baptism. Was it a holy moment? Yes, God smiled on us that day, and this was to be the first of many such events.

These are the daisies of Africa

As the day ended, we marvelled at all God continued to do. It was only later that I came to understand the full significance of that first baptism in the river. Ancestral worship was the dominant spiritual understanding among the local people, a practice that had been passed down over generations and shaped Basotho culture. This fear-based understanding held these beautiful people in such bondage. One of the fear-stories passed on to every child as they grow up, was never to enter the deepest parts of the river as there was a "demon snake" that swallowed people and caused drowning. This belief was deeply embedded in the local culture, and now we were in that exact place, baptising these very people into Jesus. Unbeknown to us, we were overcoming the very heart of wrong thinking through this powerful and obedient act of baptism.

My journal writing of that day records many of the names of those baptised, and some were the first to respond to the gospel on the opening day. One can see the joy in my words as I recall baptising Justice, an older man named Molahle, Mme Alisia and her friends, Elizabeth, Mapopina, and others. These were our people. These were God's people. These were the "daisies of Africa".

With the baptism behind us, it was our first Christmas on the farm and we were overjoyed to have the Cape Town families join us. Mac and Adien Oosthuyzen, Peter and Janis Bonney and their children were such a blessing to have for our first Christmas away from our families in Cape Town. To make it even more special, our home church in Cape Town had sent a large cardboard packing box, full of beautifully wrapped presents for us as a family. It had been a costly move to the Free State, but these many blessings were like the "dew on Mount Hermon".

Chapter 17

I WILL BUILD MY CHURCH

As we entered 1997, never would I have imagined how much God would do in us and through us over the months that lay ahead. Our family had settled quite well into farm life, but at times our longing for family and friends in Cape Town weighed heavily upon us. Loneliness was a constant companion and unwelcome guest. Heather faced the bigger battles, as I was so busy with the growing church. We were working with a very different people group, and God was continually having to adjust our ways. In addition to all the changes, our elderly farm neighbour had asked if we could take over the operation of his small dairy, and there was much to learn about cows and the milking process.

A different kind of birth!

During one of our January services, Joseph, our farm labourer, came to call me and explained that one of the cows was having difficulty calving. As soon as I could get away, I rushed to see what the problem was, only to be told that we would lose the calf if I didn't deliver it immediately. I recall questioning him about the "I". *You mean me?* And so began my long journey of handling cattle. Joseph brought a bucket of warm, soapy water and told me to wash my hands and arms. That instruction sounded ominous. Very soon, having just ministered and prayed for hundreds of eager followers, I inserted my hand and arm into this desperate cow, feeling the twisted calf and the pressure of a cow in labour. At first, I couldn't move the calf, but once I had adjusted the head and attached ropes around the calf's front legs, we slowly but surely pulled the calf free. As messy and gory as it was, it was also the most exhilarating experience to see this new little life take its first breath and almost immediately rise to its feet. The happy and relieved mother quickly licked life into her little calf with Joseph and me watching with glee and a sense of great accomplishment. I considered this new farm life God had brought Heather, the boys, and me into with wonder, and I realised that church planting was much broader in scope than I understood. I also gained a clearer understanding of the phrase, "I can do all things through Christ who strengthens me" (Philippians 4:13 NKJV). That put a smile on my face. This calf was to be the first of many calves we helped, and Heather became quite deft at injecting sick or injured animals in my absence, even though she held her breath for longer than she should have!

As the year gained momentum, Heather and I were thrilled to hear that a conversation we had with Peter Bonney had moved Janis' and his hearts, and they were starting the transition of leaving Cape Town with their children to move up to Clarens to join us. God had promised to prepare leaders for us, and He was being faithful to His word. But within the church, there were others who God had also prepared and brought to us. These included two brothers, John and Petrose Mokoena. One Sunday, I noticed these two accomplished young men standing in the doorway of the barn during the worship time. They had recently surrendered their lives to Jesus, and I observed how attentive they were. As we got to know them, we were amazed to hear another story of God initiating a great work in their hearts.

Zip guns and grace

John and Petrose had grown up in the top village at Sunnyside Farm, where our work had begun all those years before. These were small clusters of informal dwellings where the farm workers would be housed.

They had grown up with Japela (an angry older man at the time) as well as the effects of Apartheid that dominated so much of their lives. The cruelty of some white farmers had nudged them into hatred of white people, and they were getting increasingly immersed in the anti-Apartheid movement. Both John and Petrose were incredibly gifted with their hands and found an isolated area on the mountainside where they perfected the manufacture of zip guns. These improvised weapons were designed to shoot a sharpened metal object that could cause substantial injury or even kill someone. They aimed to unleash their hatred on the local farmers using these homemade weapons.

However, their sister Ntswaki had joined our church and couldn't stop talking about us and the impact of Dihlabeng Church. Their anger grew, especially when they would see me arriving to attend a small church service in their village. But God eventually softened their hearts. They couldn't stay away and travelled to the farm to visit Dihlabeng Church on a Sunday. To quote Petrose, "When I came to Dihlabeng the first time, I was shocked to see black and white people together under one roof. My political background could not comprehend what I was witnessing. And then the big surprise was to see that they truly loved one another. I wanted to discover more, and, as I did, I never looked back. My brother John, who was also involved in the political world, followed me to the church, and he was deeply moved by the unity and love he witnessed among the people. Like me, he never looked back!"

Birthdays and people-gifts

So, these God-chosen people-gifts gathered to the church in ever-increasing numbers. But there was more! As April approached, Heather began preparing for our youngest son, Adam's, second birthday. She expressed that she felt so sad about it in a way, as we had left all our family and friends in Cape Town, and it would be a quiet birthday party. God stepped in, and we discovered it coincided with hosting a team from our sister church, some four hours away in KwaZulu-Natal. We contacted them and asked if they would be willing to bring some children to Adam's party, which they agreed to enthusiastically. One of the couples who responded so willingly was Gavin and Lynne Northcote, who brought their two young girls to make up a party celebration for Adam. They were a delightful and capable couple, and very soon a deep friendship was forged, and our children became inseparable. No sooner had they said goodbye than we planned for them to revisit the farm. On their second visit, they shared with Heather and me that they were carrying a prophetic word that "God was going to uproot them from their coastal home and plant them in the heart of the country", which they had never understood until meeting us in Clarens, deep in the heart of the country. They went on to share that they felt a call to join us at Dihlabeng Church. God was building His church and, as you can imagine, Heather and I were delighted with this news.

There is so much I can write about in the early stages of 1997, but one event stands out more than any other.

Empowered from on high

At the start of the year, Wednesday evenings had a full and well-prepared programme. We were now into the third month after the church plant, and although the church was still very "raw", it continued to flourish. We set these evenings aside to train an ever-growing number of "possible leaders". I would leave the farm in my Toyota HiAce pickup truck and head to Golden Gate, some forty-five minutes away. It was the farthest point of my journey to collect all those whom I had selected for training. Each one would walk down to the main road from their village or from within the township and wait patiently for me to collect them. Then, with the pickup filled, and sometimes more, we would head back to the farm, singing the most delightful songs, like: *"Ubuhle bezulu lakhe"* (a song about 'the beauty of His heaven'). I can still hear the strains of that tune sweetly ringing in my ears. Such was the excitement, togetherness, and joy! Heather, in the meantime, would be preparing a wholesome meal for the twenty or so who would gather. It was usually a well-flavoured mince-meat dish, which was always greatly enjoyed by all. While I slowly made my way back to our home, others would also be making the journey, on foot from Lesotho, crossing the occasionally flooded Caledon River in the process. It was our rainy season, and so it wasn't surprising to have a few people drying off for the first hour of any meeting.

Those I wanted to be with

Choosing this group was an interesting and faith-filled process. I was significantly impacted by the way Jesus had gone up the mountain and, after spending much time in prayer, "He gathered those to Himself that He wanted to be with" (see Mark 3:13-15). From the birth of Dihlabeng, I consciously watched each person whom God added to us. At times, ten to twenty individuals were added each week, and so I had to do my best to get to know them as quickly as possible and try to discern the unique gifts that God was bringing. With the ever-growing congregation needing significant help, I had to gather and train a group as quickly as possible. My journal records the process: lists of names, little ticks and sadly a few crosses. Finally, with my heart settled, I had those I wanted to be with. It was a start, as small as a mustard seed, but a start. Wednesday evenings were allocated for training and subsequently started.

There are many wonderful memories of these times, memories of unbelievable commitment and passion. One young mother of four I had selected, Alice Mashinini, worked in the milking parlour on a farm some eight kilometres away from our farm. Alice was one of the very few who were Christians before the church was planted, and from the very first day she had added a vibrancy that we so needed. Sadly, her employment meant that she had to milk cows early in the morning and then until 8 p.m. each evening, making it difficult for her to participate in the leaders' training. It, however, did not deter Alice. As soon as she could leave work, she would set her course across the hills of the adjoining farms, crossing valleys and ravines, running as fast as her slight frame could carry her, even though it was as dark as anyone could imagine. Well into our meeting, our farm dogs would announce the arrival of this joyful runner, who would appear out of the pitch-black night. Often arriving soaked with sweat, she would immediately join in, never missing a beat, and she added such flavour. Such commitment. So loved.

Breaking barriers

With our home having been a place of separation in the past, a place where no Basotho person would enter unless they were a servant, we would now gather everyone eagerly together around Heather's great casserole in the kitchen. As the weeks passed, barriers slowly began to fall, allowing friendships to form and flourish. With the growing numbers, we eventually had to use the lounge area, filling every available seat. To get the conversation flowing, I would ask lots of questions. As they grew in confidence, the people began to open up. These were small mustard-seed-like beginnings, but a beginning, nonetheless.

Slowly, as the weeks progressed, I guided these dear, eager people through some of the basic teachings of their newfound faith, constantly building on the big story of God and His purposes across the earth. God had promised us much as a church, and I wanted them to know the scope of their involvement from the outset. They were ever so attentive. Some would write furiously, while others just sat and listened. Delightful songs would fill our evenings, which would, in time, become a profound form of worship. I never missed the opportunity to lay hands on each one and allow the Holy Spirit to do His work. Sadly, on many an occasion, there would be a demonic manifestation or deep wails as God touched the depths of people's hearts.

With our growing numbers, Heather and I decided to move our gatherings from the house to the barn after our evening meal. This move allowed me the freedom to follow the Holy Spirit unhindered and for lives to be made whole as God worked out His purposes. Although the barn was a little dark and cavernous at times, we set out a quadrangle of hay bales and used an old red carpet to fill the middle. We loved it. It was ours.

God stories

My diary records that Sunday, 12th January 1997, was a very special day. I wrote, *"Today was our most effective meeting – we seemed to achieve so much."* My writings continued to highlight the involvement of many of these leaders-in-training, as well as the incredible presence of the Holy Spirit. A lady from a nearby farm who had been experiencing nightly demonic experiences, testified how she had been healed of an ear problem the week before, and that she had been set free from these nightly activities. The congregation received this news with great joy! And so, this Wednesday's leaders' meeting was filled with testimony and joy. It was very clear that something extraordinary had started. The following Sunday, our numbers swelled to two hundred and fifty adults and, once again, there were "God-stories" in abundance as people shared how God was working in their lives. I recorded one young man's testimony: "Last week I came up for prayer because I couldn't find work. The next morning, Monday, I got a job! I've decided to give the church my first pay packet!" My diary records: *"The church exploded with praise!"* These were exciting days, filled with many accounts of God sovereignly touching lives.

Pentecost again!

Now it was Wednesday again. God was at work, and I knew what I needed to teach. Throughout the week, I had been busy preparing a detailed teaching entitled: "Empowered from on high – baptised in the Holy Spirit." Knowing how an encounter with the Holy Spirit had so radically changed me and so many others, I anticipated transformation in these lives as well. The long ride to the farm that evening was full of expectation, and we squeezed as many as we could into the pickup, commonly known as a *"bakkie"* in our nation. Men piled into the canopy-protected rear, with as many ladies as possible squashed into the double-cab section. There was a lot to celebrate over dinner, and then we made our way across the yard to the barn. The bales awaited, and we settled in for what promised to be another action-packed leaders' gathering. But nothing could have prepared me for what I was about to witness.

I explained that the evening's teaching was one of the most important that they would hear. I detailed the nature of what I hoped for, explaining once again the enormous task that

God has set before us in reaching the far ends of the earth. For most, there was no understanding of what "reaching the ends of the earth" meant, as most had never even crossed the borders of their village or town. I understood this much later, yet it is what God had declared over us through prophetic promises.

Before beginning the teaching, I asked everyone to stand and invited the Holy Spirit to begin "gathering us in". There was a "sweetness" to the atmosphere in that barn, and immediately, I could sense God was at work. Ntswaki and Mapopina began to sing the most beautiful Zulu song, "*Tsolela Moya*".

> *Tsolela moea oa hau Jesu*
> [Let your power come, Jesus]
> *Lipelong tsa rona Jesu*
> [into our hearts]
> *Tsolela moea oa hau Jesu*
> [Let your power come, Jesus]

The voices ebbed and flowed as the ladies took the lead, and the men added bass and volume. Hands reached out, and I knew we were touching something different. I've heard worship described as a place where we can enter "the new creation, a place where Jesus has ascended to" and, that night, it felt as if we had left that rather cavernous barn and we were right there with Him. Acts chapter 2 describes the moment the Spirit arrived among Jesus' disciples as "suddenly". We were about to experience a "suddenly" moment.

Suddenly!

While we were still singing, the Spirit came! Such was the outpouring on us as leaders that evening that all but three of us were left standing! These young, eager, beautiful people were so powerfully touched that they were all thrown backwards, over the bales behind them, each hitting the concrete floor with a great "slap!" It was as if a great "bucket of blessing" had been poured out into the middle of the hay-bale quadrangle, causing a great "splash" that powerfully threw these leaders backwards, tumbling over the bales. Like those who received this blessing from on high at Pentecost, they all began speaking in tongues, overflowing with joy, tears, and cries of delight. This encounter lasted for quite some time, and at one point, I had to stop Elias, one of the few who hadn't been filled, from slapping people on the cheek to bring them around. He had never experienced anything like this before and didn't understand what was happening. I explained what we were seeing and encouraged him to join in and pray over them, but the interesting thing was that Elias never allowed the Spirit to impact his life. Despite three years of trying so hard to build him in, Elias finally left our work, which was a sad time for me.

I never got to do my teaching on that memorable Wednesday evening. Such was the intensity of God's outpouring that we finally had to lift many of these newly filled individuals into the pickup and take them home. Arriving at some of the villages later that night was an interesting experience. Parents and family members looked on suspiciously as we arrived at their homes, and I had to explain: "They are not drunk as you suppose!"

My diary for Wednesday 22nd January records:

> *Pentecost again!*
> *They received the baptism of the Spirit!*
> *Mapopina was "blown away".*
> *Alice was wailing!*
> *Steven delivered!*
> *Thank You, Lord!*

How can one ever capture effectively on paper what happened that night? Peter had declared some two thousand years before what God had promised:

> *"Repent and be baptised, every one of you, in the name of Jesus Christ for the forgiveness of your sins. And you will receive the gift of the Holy Spirit. The promise is for you and your children and for all who are far off – for all whom the Lord our God will call."*
>
> (Acts 2:38-39 NIV)

God had not forgotten the far-off Basotho people.

Chapter 18

WHO WILL YOU BECOME?

Having experienced God in such a tangible way, the developing leaders of Dihlabeng Church continued to prosper in every way. There was a new confidence, and it felt as if everyone now belonged both in understanding and in commitment to God's purposes. Meetings were filled with extraordinary manifestations of the Holy Spirit, and there was always an immediate response to the gospel of grace. Testimonies of healing were a great encouragement for us to continue pressing into God and trusting Him in this unusual church setting. Recently, I spoke with an elderly member of Dihlabeng Church, Mme Ntatoleng, who was there from the very beginning, and we reminisced about the first time we met. On that day, just before the Sunday meeting was about to begin, I was at the front of the dusty, hay-bale-filled barn and, as I turned around, I was surprised to find Mme Ntatoleng approaching me on her knees, slowly shuffling towards me on the dusty floor. It was her first Sunday with us, and I was taken aback by her position, believing she was approaching the "Pastor" in a subservient and humble way.

Stepping forward, I took her arms, lifted her to her feet and explained, "We don't do that in this church! Yes, I lead, but we're a family, there is no need to come to me on your knees." Mme Ntatoleng and I laughed as we recalled that moment so many years ago, but then she began to shake her head in disagreement and offered me a very different explanation of what had happened. She had heard about the church and how so many were finding peace, belonging, and healing. She arranged to travel to church on the tractor and trailer from one of the adjoining farms and came to seek God for healing, as she had lost the use of her legs for several years, only being able to move around on her knees. In stunned silence, I looked at her as she explained that, as I lifted her from the floor, God restored her legs and healed her completely, after which she walked back to her chosen spot and sat down! Healed! Completely healed! Hearing this was news to me and showed me that God was doing far more than I realised. That was the atmosphere of the gatherings in those early days. Despite our humble, hot, sweaty, and raw barn filled with people who could barely give anything in the offering, God was pouring out His grace . . . God was pouring out His grace on these chosen people through a very inadequate and inexperienced leader. Each time Mme Ntatoleng and I meet, we laugh as we recall God's goodness, how He healed her and that she was not being subservient but in need of healing – oh Lord! She is still in the church; she never misses a meeting at Dihlabeng but still asks me whenever she can to pray for her now "older knees".

Farm life amid revival

With the gospel proving to be such good news for the poor, Dihlabeng was now taking shape. Three young adults, Catherine, Jason, and Samantha, arrived from different parts of the world to serve us for a year and joined our ever-maturing team of leaders. The Bonney family were about to come from Cape Town, having sold their home and packed their belongings. The Northcote family was also in the process of moving. God was gathering His team, and Dihlabeng was abuzz with activity. For Heather and me, farm life, three small boys, and many surprises continued to keep us busy. During that time, I began to teach the church about giving and generosity. We made giving to special offerings a regular event during the year, allowing people to bring whatever they could manage. It wasn't always money, and so we received the most amazing gifts. One lady put a plastic carry bag into the big basket one morning, and it wasn't long before the bag started wriggling. Finally, a chicken's head popped out of a hole in the bag! Heather bought it. Beautiful brooms made from local grasses were a common gift, and Heather bought them too! And then, a small piglet, pink with dark markings. Heather bought it as well! We laughed so much as a church because everyone knew that Mme Heather loved animals, and the offering would "grow" if they put an animal in the basket.

The piglet quickly settled into the farmyard, squealing with delight whenever he managed to steal something to eat. The dogs grew more and more annoyed with him as he would charge at their bowls during dinner, knocking them aside and eagerly diving into their food, making loud pig-like noises. As he got older, he became quite unruly. The situation peaked when we came home one day to find him lying on his back on our sofa, fast asleep and snoring loudly. Eventually, we decided to give him to a family in need.

Shorn the Sheep was an interesting addition too. Shorn didn't arrive through the offer, but we found him abandoned and injured in the field. The boys were delighted to have this little lamb in the house and bottle-fed him until he grew round and healthy. Whenever he could, he would run inside to the kitchen to see if there was anything to nibble. When caught, we'd shout at him, and he would turn and run on his little stiletto hooves, dropping sheep pellets in great quantities down the passage. Such was farm life. Shorn was eventually given to a lady in the church who managed a nearby farm, where he lived out his days as a most lovely and friendly companion. He enjoyed evening walks, a cosy pen, and his new family; they even bought him a friend. He lived a long sheep-life, and Shorn's headstone can be seen on a farm near Golden Gate.

While I'm about it, it would be good to remember Billy the Blesbok. One late Sunday afternoon, we heard the cries of a newborn calf coming from a distant field. Taking the older boys, I went to investigate, and we gathered up this tiny little newborn deer. His mother had rejected him, but he soon became an integral part of the Oliver household. The boys took turns to feed him, and he loved the two dogs, believing that he was one of them. Slowly but surely, Billy grew to be a majestic ram and, whenever we walked on the farm, Billy was sure to show off all his jumping, pronking, and bucking moves. He chased the dogs and was a great deal of fun to have around until he reached maturity. Bucks have a very clear hierarchy in the herd, and Billy decided that he was the alpha male, and he was number two in our household. It meant Heather was never able to hold my hand as we walked on the farm or even walk alongside me. If she did, Billy would interject and turn to face Heather, horns down, making it very clear that she needed to drop behind him. It was even more difficult for our three boys, as he was now larger than they were, and he expected them to fall into line as well. Even so, he was great fun. He would join us for outdoor *braais* and lie peacefully on our front lawn. I remember sitting up against him and even taking a nap, leaning peacefully against this delightful animal. Sadly, a visiting game ranger advised us that he would eventually become very dangerous as he got older, and so we relocated him to a nearby game farm. We missed Billy.

Reshaping for gospel advance

As the year maintained its never-ceasing momentum, I found myself questioning much of what we were doing. Revival settings can be very exhilarating, but they are also messy and unpredictable. Some of my questions about whether I was fulfilling the call of God and building something that would last were fuelled by disappointments where potential leaders would fail miserably and cause untold sadness among us. Yet the church was now taking shape, and, even though we worked hard to ensure Sundays were filled with good teaching and the Holy Spirit's activity, it was time to start building. We were very isolated in terms of receiving ongoing input from others, and so a lot depended on my pioneering and leadership gift. It was to become a weakness a few years later. I will write about it in future chapters.

When God planted the first seed of church planting in my heart, He also began giving me several specific promises. I made it a habit to record these, and I carried them in my heart, just as I had read that biblical leaders of old had done. So, when the time came to move and plant Dihlabeng Church, my heart was full of promises. They shaped me, directed me, released faith in me, and I was always careful not to despise the simplest of words. To my detriment, I also shared my dreams and beliefs about what Dihlabeng Church would eventually look like, and this was not always well received. After receiving one rather discouraging response, I decided to take some time and seek the Lord to find out what He desired of us. Sitting on the rocky outcrop behind our home, I poured my heart out before the Lord, feeling rather sorry for myself. It was during this time that God spoke to me, gently yet clearly. "Who will you become? How will Dihlabeng Church be remembered one day? Will it be for your mission? Will it be for church planting? Will it be your work among the poor? Who will you become? These were tender and kind words that challenged my heart to find the answers.

Over a few weeks, I filled my journal with thoughts and details as they came to mind. I also devoted myself to studying the New Testament churches and immediately understood that every church was quite unique in its own right; it certainly wasn't a one-size-fits-all sort of programme. The Corinthians were known for the outworking of the gifts of the Spirit and a measure of immaturity, the Philippians for their great love for one another and their ownership of the apostolic call, the Bereans for their steadfastness in the Word of God, and so forth. Slowly but surely, understanding came, and I sketched out the future.

However, the confusing part for me was that I had set a very "high bar of expectation" for what Dihlabeng Church would become, a work among the poor that redefines church and reaches the ends of the earth. The promises had shaped my thinking that we would be a church that sent brothers and sisters to the ends of the earth, enabling us to reach the unreached. I believed that God had called us to overcome poverty and to empower the poor to participate fully in the world mission. I further believed we would share in resourcing the nations as we planted churches in far-off nations. These were my desires, but reality was a very different thing. At the time, we were gathering around three hundred on a Sunday, the vast majority coming from seriously impoverished homes, where most could only afford one meal a day. Education was lacking, and our offerings rarely exceeded R2,000 a month, and we only had two vehicles among us in the church. Furthermore, we were in the most isolated and remote part of our nation, with no outside influence whatsoever, and most people in our country, South Africa, had no idea where Clarens was. That was the reality. How then could Dihlabeng Church ever reach my "high bar" of expectation?

As I worked through all these positive and negative thoughts, I finally settled on one clear thought: above everything, I wanted Dihlabeng Church to be a community that truly loved God and loved one another. That would be our goal and starting point. For the rest, we would have to keep believing and trusting God.

The harvest was ripe

With this newfound clarity and the arrival of some of the Bonney family in July of that year, Dihlabeng Church took on a whole new flavour. We were very focused and started to settle into a new confidence. Looking back, it is staggering to see how many were getting saved over those months in 1997. At times, my journals record forty-plus people making first-time commitments on a Sunday, and two weeks later, I excitedly recorded that in one week, eighty-four had taken hold of the gospel of grace! As we couldn't transport everyone, we started meetings on the farms around Clarens, making it easier for everyone to experience this new wave of grace. It also provided my developing leadership with the opportunity to preach and teach, and very quickly, we could see that God had handpicked some significant gifts among the people.

Our first church plant

Sadly, our window of opportunity to receive our brothers and sisters from across the river in Lesotho had finally closed. One Sunday, a well-armed army and police force arrived and arrested everyone from Lesotho. It was a traumatic experience for many, and our dear friends filled two prison cells at the local border town prison. They were held for an entire week in the cells before being deported across the border. It changed everything for the church, and the following week we planted our first church next to the river below the Thabakholo village. There was no preparation for the church plant, but it did feel very New Testament in nature as it got planted out of a scattering. We quickly adjusted to the new rhythms of church life, holding morning meetings in the barn, followed by afternoon meetings alongside the river under the willow trees.

Life never stood still. It was dynamic and fast-paced for such a rural setting. Sundays were very full days, and on several occasions the meeting at the riverside was interrupted by donkeys, cows, and even lightning strikes that made everyone run for cover. This was the church God had chosen to reach the ends of the earth, which was difficult to correlate with what was happening on the ground. Despite all the difficulties, we continued to see much of God's grace and treasured each of the joint baptism services we would hold down at the river, where the riverbanks would be awash with people and colour. God was doing something special, and we did our best to follow obediently.

Chapter 19

STANDING ON OTHERS' SHOULDERS

If one has ever had the privilege of attending a good stage production, one very quickly appreciates that there is an army of people making it all happen behind what you see in front of you. The actors are centre stage, but behind the curtains, many committed unseen people are ensuring the production flows smoothly and is a success. When I read my journals and take the time to reflect on all that God has done, it's easy to be inspired by the many who came to Christ and the numerous significant miracles we witnessed during these early months. However, I'm so glad that I also kept details of our interaction with several outstanding people who believed in Heather and me, and played such a key part in our success at the time, even though they too were in the background and hidden at times.

Jeff and Viv

This group included the likes of Jeff and Viv Kidwell, who were now in their fourth year of establishing The Bay Community Church in Cape Town. Having sent us off a year earlier, they continued to play a vital role in keeping us grounded and focused on Jesus. Their friendship and love were invaluable. Communication was not what it is today, and long landline phone calls kept us in touch regularly.

Our move to Clarens was challenging for the four of us, as well as for The Bay Community Church. We were devoted to The Bay and to Jeff and Viv, who had played a vital role in our Christian lives. Now, we found ourselves fourteen hours apart, and God was guiding us on paths that were very different from The Bay Church in Cape Town. As time went on, I became increasingly drawn to Simon Pettit's apostolic vision and found myself less dependent on Jeff and the influence that he and The Bay Church had on us. Still, they consistently supported us by sending teams and providing resources at crucial moments.

These kinds of changes are never easy for anyone. However, what I most value and appreciate about Jeff and Viv is that they always sought to understand God's purposes for us and aligned themselves with those purposes, even when it was difficult for them. This selflessness allowed us to remain deeply connected over the years, celebrating our successes and the advancement of the Kingdom, while also mourning during times of loss, especially when Viv sadly passed away after a long illness. To this day, my three boys will say that Jeff is one of their favourite people, which is a testament to the positive impact that he and Viv had on their lives.

Simon Pettit – a mighty oak

Simon Pettit arrived in South Africa at a pivotal moment in the nation's history, and his sharp mind and effervescent personality soon began to shape all our churches. Once he had settled into leading Jubilee Church in Cape Town, which included a name change and a significant move for the church community, Simon's apostolic message began to create a profound "apostolic wake", and we were immediately drawn into the dynamic biblical nature of his vision. I recall listening to him paint a broad picture of God's purposes and feeling my heart burn with passion, longing to play my part. On one occasion, I can remember saying to God, "I don't fully understand the gift you have given Simon, but I want to ask you for some of it! I want to do what he does!" I believe God heard that passionate and innocent prayer, honouring it many years later. He was highly inspiring and so helpful in the complex political situation we found ourselves in, living in South Africa.

In late 1997, I travelled to Kenya with Simon and spent ten days bouncing around in an old Land Rover on the Great African Highway, watching him shape the Kenyan church leaders and their church communities. I didn't fully understand at the time, but Simon was laying an apostolic foundation in the lives of these dear friends, and I filled my journal with this fresh teaching that continues to shape my life to this day. I watched Simon with people, I watched him in worship, and I watched him when he was so ill for three days, never once complaining or pulling back from the extraordinary demands placed on him. The apostle Paul of the New Testament was able to speak so fondly of his spiritual son, Timothy, saying that "he will remind you of my ways which are in Christ" (1 Corinthians 4:17 NASB). That rather gruelling trip to Kenya gave me a front-row seat to watch and learn Simon's "ways", and it was ever so helpful as I believe I was "baptised" into his ways.

I'm so grateful for the nine years I was able to lead under Simon's oversight before his untimely death in 2005. Even though he only visited us twice in Clarens over those years, we understood his ways and built as best as we could under his large apostolic umbrella. At times when I know I disappointed him, his big heart would draw me in, and even to this day, I can still feel that large hand of his, squeezing my shoulder with deep affection. He had a significant impact on us.

On Simon's first visit to Clarens, I gathered our developing leaders in the small local golf club building for the evening, as it was one of the very few venues in our little, undeveloped town. Most of the young leaders sat on the carpet as Simon passionately unpacked the experience the disciples had the day Jesus found them fishing. The story recounts their extraordinary catch that day, so large that they had to call on other fishing boats for assistance. Referencing the significant breakthrough we were seeing in Dihlabeng Church and the vast opportunity that lay before us, Simon encouraged us that we were not alone in this isolated place of Clarens and that we could call on the other churches in our family to help with the big catch. He lifted our expectations about the extraordinary work God had called our unusual church to, and instructed us to be a people of faith and obedience. Thereafter, he prayed for us, one at a time. God moved significantly and then, turning to me, he placed both hands on my chest. As he prayed, I felt he was praying knowingly, using the words, "Lord, I ask that what you have placed in me you would impart to Steve right now, in a measure according to your purposes. Steve, go and do the apostolic work God's called you to do." It was a special moment for me on that cold evening at the golf club. It was also a lesson on how fathers can provide such encouragement and affirmation to their sons. I miss Simon, as I'm sure we all do. He was a beautiful gift to the church, and his impact continues to produce gospel fruit among us.

Your friend, Ray

In researching the details for this book, I came across times in the planting of Dihlabeng Church that were incredibly difficult for Heather and me. Cross-cultural ministry can be challenging and isolating at times, and when you face the constant pressures of working among the impoverished, it can be pretty overwhelming. I came across an entry I had made in my journal, which occurred right in the middle of the season when many responded to the gospel and the church was flourishing. Many, many were turning to Jesus, and it was a dream come true for any church. Yet, I recorded this: *"The past two weeks have been some of the most difficult we have faced. We have just R200 to our name, and it is causing great pressure at home."* These times of extreme pressure often coincide with special family events, such as birthdays. As a husband and father, I felt pretty defeated at times. When we did receive any form of finance, there were so many areas of need that our family often came last, adding enormous pressure to our home life.

One of the reasons we got through those difficult and stretching times was the ownership of our vision that Ray and Sue Lowe showed. Through their faithful church family based in Biggin Hill, Kent, England, they would surprise us, and a timely fax communication would arrive from the church secretary, Julie, stating that they had collected a gift for us and it was on its way. Biggin Hill Christian Fellowship showed such ownership of our work in Clarens, which was a lifeline in those early days. However, it wasn't so much the greatly appreciated finances that meant so much to us, but instead how Ray and Sue owned the vision of Dihlabeng Church.

With all its unusual complexities, Ray seemed to have the ability to see through the poverty, the simplicity, and the educational challenges and focus on the beauty of what God was doing among us. Never once did he waver in his appreciation for the fact that God would use our isolated rural church to impact nations. For those who know this colourful man, they will recall that he would ask the most direct questions at times, making our Basotho leaders laugh with joy. I believe he and Sue were part of the reason we saw the "walls of division" come tumbling down. Their deep relationship with our church was best showcased when they celebrated their fiftieth wedding anniversary while in Clarens. Moved by God, we seated them on the stage, and the entire church filed forward to honour them with small gifts on this very special occasion. It was excruciatingly humbling for Ray and Sue to receive gifts from the poorest of the poor, but such a fitting example of the church's love for them. Many tears flowed that day.

For Heather and me, Ray made sure we had fun! Life was not simple for us over those years, and so Ray did everything he could to ensure we enjoyed life to the full. He would prod, provoke, and challenge us, with Sue interjecting regularly with a firm, "Ray!" Faithful, fun, and never dull is how I would describe those years of journeying with Ray and Sue. In every communication to us, Ray would conclude with a closing statement, "Your friend, Ray." He meant it, and we knew it.

Gary and Nicky – faithful and true

And finally, Gary and Nicky Welsh. In 1997, Gary and Nicky asked if they could come and visit us after our Cape Town conference. We didn't know them very well, but we were happy to have friends visit us in our home. Poor Gary and Nicky! On their first of many visits to us over the years, they arrived in the coldest weather imaginable. In the morning, Gary had put on nearly every piece of clothing he had brought with him; they almost froze. To add to it, our old farmhouse was still in a very raw state and, much to our embarrassment, two of the largest rats ran around in the roof all night, sounding like giant wild beasts. Gary was aghast and made his feelings known about the "wild animals in the roof", and we sure laughed a lot.

This dear couple showed great compassion for our church community and did everything they could to support and promote our success. I still have a Matt Redman CD they brought as a gift, saying, "We're sure you guys don't get much of the latest of anything living here, so we thought you'd like some recently released worship." When it came to conferences, Nicky would break all the rules for me, ensuring that none of my leaders were left out, despite having little to no funding. She would giggle when asked if I could add one or two more to my list, and not once was I refused a place. These are small details, but the impact on the development of our leaders was huge. And Gary, I could call on him for anything. How grateful we are for this couple who laid down so much and faced such difficulties in their later lives – we're so thankful to God for His healing work in Nicky in recent times.

The gospel was never meant to be lived out in isolation but always in community. I am deeply grateful for the people God placed around us and for the unwavering support they all provided during those early years. Would we have succeeded without them? Looking back, I don't think so.

Chapter 20

FORCEFUL ADVANCE

The impact of Dihlabeng Church began to be felt across the area as God mobilised His newly transformed and gathered people in Dihlabeng Church. We continued to witness a steady wave of salvation throughout the region, which was celebrated with great joy in the church. It was a rural church in its rawest form – sometimes washed out by rain, experiencing powerful moves of God the following Sunday, witnessing multiple healings, with frozen keyboards as the winter temperatures dropped well below freezing in the barn, and facing the constant challenges of extreme poverty. However, as 1998 began, we found ourselves with a renewed vision for the new year. Initially, I introduced a biblical understanding of the Breaking of Bread for the first time, and then we partook of this great blessing together with enthusiasm. My journal records that we had a large gathering in the building, and everyone listened with great attentiveness as our well-instructed leadership team served the community. It was a precious moment. We had become one, and we celebrated it with great reverence. Jesus had become more than just a saviour; He was our Lord, and we honoured Him in a very special way.

The ends of the earth start with Africa!

Over the initial years, we received many visitors, and we never missed an opportunity to be trained and discipled by them. Even though I was leading, this was such helpful training for me, and the church flourished. It was at this time that I introduced the church to our first world map. Gathering the three young students, we gave them a length of calico cloth, and they set to work painting the nations across this three-metre-wide white material in bright green. I introduced our mission field to the church with great enthusiasm and fanfare, only to be surprised by the lack of enthusiasm over what I thought was a great vision-casting moment. Over the week, I chatted to the leaders and found out that education was the issue. Very few understood the continents and nations as one would typically understand them had they learned about them in school. I gathered the student team, and this time, we painted the continent of Africa, with a big red dot depicting Clarens. The response from the congregation was immediate, and so we decided to tackle Africa as our first task. These were precious moments and a constant reminder that "God chooses the foolish things to confound the world".

Leadership in covenant

Gavin and Lynne Northcote had now arrived and were settling into country life and their unusual church. Gavin's worship and leadership gifts added a new dimension to the church, and one could feel the impact within the church community. It proved invaluable as we introduced multi-lingual songs. Lynne's diverse gift mix was also greatly appreciated, and she filled numerous gaps in our growing church. At times, it felt as if there was nothing this valuable couple could not do, which added to the maturity of our fledgling church. Very quickly, new opportunities for us to minister in other towns arose, and participation reached an all-time high. Sundays were exciting and exhausting, and they often spilt over into smaller meetings around the area during the week.

It was in this exciting season that Gavin Northcote, Justice Mofokeng, Peter Bonney, and I became the bedrock of the church, carrying the load with endless energy and outstanding commitment. In this time of significant advance, the four of us made the humblest commitment to God and to one another. Not knowing all that lay before us but understanding that God had entrusted something very special to us, we decided to take on the task before us with a true sense of ownership. We decided that one day, when we were nearing the end of our active ministry in the church, maybe a little greyer and older, we would still be found to be loving God, fully committed to the church in the same way as when we started, and still enjoying a deep friendship with one another. It was a sweet, innocent, but weighty commitment, one that we treasured in our hearts.

Thirty years and counting

As I write this account, Dihlabeng Church is about to enter its thirtieth year since its inception. Wonderfully, Justice, Pete, Gavin, and I remain together in God, and our friendship continues; our passion for the church is evident every week at Dihlabeng Church. We're quite a bit older now, but we can boast that God has been faithful to His promises and His presence, and we're in awe of all He has done over the years. I'm so grateful for that simple yet powerful decision we made so many years ago. These three are exceptional men, and I believe this region owes them an outstanding debt.

Lesotho flourishes

With our work in the small community meetings on farms around Clarens flourishing, many continued to turn to Christ. Equally so, our fledgling church community meeting alongside the river in Lesotho was also gaining strength. In fact, we managed to purchase a small piece of land and obtained permission to build our own facility, which was greeted with great excitement by our Lesotho brothers and sisters. But it was not without opposition.

To travel to the small town of Clarens from our farm, we would take a mile-and-a-half journey up a challenging gravel road, especially in the rainy season. One morning, as I left our home, I got about halfway up the gravel track when I saw an army vehicle parked alongside the road. As I drew near, I was a bit surprised to find two army officers physically abusing a local Basotho man. The officers were both white South African men, and I got out of my car and asked them what they were doing. They responded, saying that the man receiving the beating had crossed over from Lesotho illegally and had not shown proper respect for the law. I interjected that this did not allow them to mishandle him, and they had no rights except to arrest him and take him into detention, where he would be charged for illegal entry into South Africa. Their response was not favourable, but the beating did stop. I returned to my car, but I knew there would be retribution, as they were certainly not pleased with my intervention.

Several months before this unfortunate situation, a young and courageous English couple, Andrew and Helen Baddeley, had joined our team for two years. Meanwhile, Andrew and John Mokoena had taken on a significant amount of responsibility across the river in our growing Lesotho congregation. With the border now closed to our Lesotho family, we were granted informal permission by a local military commander to cross the river for Sunday services, rather than many of them crossing into South Africa, as had been the case before. Two weeks after the incident on my farm road, I joined John Mokoena and Andrew Baddeley for the afternoon trek across the river and the Lesotho service. It was a spectacular day alongside the river, and a colourful display of local dress greeted us as we enjoyed the shade of the numerous willow trees that line the banks of the Mohokare River. These were always special times, and we so enjoyed the fellowship with our Basotho family based in Habafokeng, Lesotho.

Ambushed!

After the meeting had concluded around mid-afternoon, John, Andrew, and I began the slow two-kilometre uphill climb from the river, rejoicing in all we had seen in Lesotho. Halfway home, the veld grass erupted as ten fully camouflaged and armed soldiers rose out of the grass, pointing automatic weapons at us. As you can imagine, we got a massive shock and were told to raise our hands. Stepping forward, the two officers I had confronted on the farm road explained that we had crossed the border illegally and were now under arrest. As much as I protested, I realised that I was not going to get my way and, after being loaded into an army vehicle, we were taken to the nearby town of Fouriesburg, where we were booked by a rather surprised local policeman and placed in a cell with around twenty other men. Our belts, laces, and possessions were taken away, but to my amusement, they let me keep my small Nokia mobile phone, giving new meaning to the term "cell phone".

When we were arrested, I managed to persuade the officers to let me inform Heather that we were being taken into custody and would appear before the magistrate the following day. As you can imagine, she was far from pleased.

The prison cell was something else entirely. More than twenty men lined the walls, lounging in a haze of camaraderie and smoke. Marijuana joints were passed freely from hand to hand, and a thick cloud of smoke hovered about a metre above the floor, like a ceiling of fog. We were welcomed like old friends, and quickly found a spot against the wall, doing our best to stay beneath the cloud of smoke.

Despite the circumstances, the atmosphere was surprisingly cheerful. I couldn't help but smile when one of the inmates greeted me by name, most likely someone who had once attended Dihlabeng Church. That small recognition, in such an unexpected place, added a strange warmth to an otherwise sobering night.

It was Sunday, and there was nobody on duty with much authority to do anything about our situation, so we were stuck. However, Heather did not take no for an answer! Late that night, after sharing the gospel with a rather inebriated congregation in our cell, we heard the jingling of the keys rattling against the steel door. John, Andrew and I were summoned from among our new congregation. There were great cheers from our fellow prisoners and many goodbyes, especially from two young men Andrew had led to the Lord. When we reached the charge office, Heather stood with some of our church members and a large pink pillow in her arms. They had managed to locate the station commander at his home and had arranged for our release, which was good news for us, even though we were now in a fairly happy state of mind. With the volume of smoke in the cell, it was impossible not to join in! After being released, the three of us were instructed to appear in court at 10 a.m. the next morning, which we duly did. I did ask Heather what the large pink pillow was for, only to be told that she wanted me to be comfortable if I had to spend the night there. How sweet! I'm not sure what my fellow inmates would have thought about that.

It was Monday. When the magistrate arrived, one could see that it was Monday by his demeanour, and I thought we were in for a life sentence when he looked across his rather packed courtroom. His bushy, dark eyebrows were so thick and menacing that I must admit, I wondered if he had ever smiled in his life; it did not bode well for our hearing. Two misdemeanours were swiftly dealt with, and then the three of us were called to the dock, standing shoulder to shoulder in the raised wooden structure. The magistrate took a long, intense look at us, wondering what on earth this multi-cultural criminal group had done in his sleepy little town to result in our arrest. With great theatrical pose, the prosecutor read out the details of the charge against us, and it sounded quite intimidating. I had told John and Andrew not to open their mouths, if possible, especially Andrew, who had the most beautiful English accent and was dependent on a very special visa to be with us in Clarens.

Go and do what God has called you to do!

After reading out the charges, the magistrate asked if I had anything to say. That's not what you say to a pastor! For the next forty-five minutes, I shared Heather's and my journey, how we had left Cape Town with a call from God to "the daisies of Africa", how we were instructed by God to bring hope to the hopeless, and build His kingdom in this region. On all accounts, I seemed to do quite well as the courtroom was very attentive, and my story seemed to be quite compelling. As I closed, the prosecutor explained that he felt that this did not require a charge, but merely a warning to never cross the border in this illegal manner again. Just before the magistrate slammed his gavel onto the counter, he looked at me and said, "Pastor Oliver, please come to my chambers." With the crash of his gavel, the case was closed.

A duty police officer led me to the rear of the building to the magistrate's chambers, where I found him removing his robes. I was instructed to sit in an old leather government-issue chair in his dingy office. Without a smile, he asked me why I had never been to see him before, which I didn't quite understand. He went on to explain that he had immense local authority and could have helped us with what God had called us to do. I was transfixed as I listened attentively to this rather gruff but sincere man. He then asked me where I lived and many other details, which he duly wrote on his legal pad. After a long period of silence, he handed me a letter, and I was instructed to go to the local government border-control point, where I was to present it. "I have just established the 'Kromdraai Farm Border Crossing' on your farm," he declared! He did smile! Shaking my hand, he explained that all the relevant documents would be in place and that we would now have a legal border post on our farm, where visas would be issued and placed in our passports, allowing up to six members of our church to cross the river at any time of day. "Go and do what God has called you to do!"

"If God is for you, who can be against you!" (see Romans 8:31). For two and a half years, the miraculously provided border post on our farm adjoining Lesotho, remained open. It allowed us to cross at will and lay a strong biblical foundation in the church in Lesotho. Our legal gateway became even more fun when some friends of ours asked if Heather and I could provide a home for two horses, and I was thrilled to take possession of Flame, a lovely brown Basotho Pony mare. Most Saturdays, with my passport in hand, I would ride Flame across the farm, through the river and up into the foothills of Lesotho to meet with our leaders or, most often, with the chief of the area adjacent to our farm. He lived in Haparamente, which is a forty-five-minute ride. On arrival, this elderly Basotho man, Ntate Paramente, would take Flame by the reins and lead her to a cool spot where he would provide the horse with some juicy leaves from his vegetable garden. Then we would sit for a few hours to discuss the role of the church in his area, which sadly didn't result in much action. Even so, those were magical moments that I will treasure for a lifetime. My ride would often be greeted with great cheers from the villagers and even some laughter by the younger men, who found my ungainly riding style quite amusing.

Miraculous provision – rivers rise!

With the continued number of people accepting Christ and his Lordship, it was time to head to the Mohokare River again for our second baptism. Seventy new believers were ready for baptism, and our team selected a suitable Sunday. Sadly, we had been going through a very dry, challenging drought, and the summer rains had all but abated. As a result, the Mohokare River was hardly flowing, except for a tiny trickle in the centre of the riverbed.

On the morning of the baptism service, I took three young men, James, Stephen, and Emmanuel, down to the river in my pickup truck. We selected a location where we could excavate a sizable hole in the riverbed for the baptisms. We hoped that as the morning progressed, the trickle of water would slowly fill the well-dug hole in the base of the river. I left the three enthusiastic young men on the riverbank and headed back up the dusty track to the barn to prepare for the morning service. Slowly, our joyful community began to grow, worship began, and I knew we were in for a significant morning. After a brief Bible message focusing on the upcoming baptism, we gathered the congregation. With much singing, chatter, and celebration, the colourful parade began as everyone made their way down to the river.

I jumped into the pickup truck and drove ahead, wanting to ensure that my trusted men had prepared well for the upcoming baptisms. On arrival at the river, I was annoyed to see them stand up out of the grass where they had been sunning themselves. They picked up my frustration but smiled in response, showing a substantial measure of haughtiness. James pointed towards the river and walked with me to the edge of the bank, which was a few metres above the river level. Beneath me was a river of water, three-feet deep, clean, and flowing steadily. I looked at James for an explanation, and he joyfully explained that, as they stepped into the river, the water level slowly began to rise until it was three-feet deep! He went on to say that he had no explanation for where the water had come from, knowing we were in the upper catchment of the river and there hadn't been a drop of rain. Silenced by the hand of God, what provision. It was surely to be a day of miracles.

It was a glorious day, filled with gratitude, worship, and togetherness. As the last members were baptised, the river slowly receded, and by an hour later it was just a trickle once again.

Wrong choices

The pace of growth and the influence of the church meant that we were constantly faced with considerable decisions that weighed heavily at times. The incredible healing and other miracles, as well as the life of the church, began to have a profound impact on the local white South African population, and their numbers within the church grew. Even though we were enjoying a post-Apartheid era in South Africa, our local people groups were still deeply divided by skin colour, history, and economic disparity. We were thrilled to start impacting white South Africans, but it wasn't without difficulties. For instance, worship in the local Sesotho language was simple, energy-sapping, and repetitive in terms of content, resulting in murmuring from our English-speaking members. Our preaching was aimed at an oral culture and therefore involved many stories and "little meat", as some began to suggest. However, it was this more affluent group of people who were the backbone of the church financially, and we were very grateful for their support and resourcefulness.

What started as a small suggestion eventually evolved into a more regular request presented to our leadership team. Several English-speaking families asked if we could begin an English-speaking service that didn't involve translation and where we could sing more appropriate songs. The "noise" grew louder until we relented and eventually started a more culturally relevant service for the English- and Afrikaans-speaking people groups. I was grateful to the twenty Basotho leaders who also committed themselves to this new service, helping to maintain our multi-cultural flavour.

That meant Sundays were very busy, with an early service in English, a second service in Sesotho, followed by the meeting at the river. Simon Pettit later advised us to relocate our meetings to the town, and, after considerable difficulty, we found two suitable venues for the two Clarens-based services. We soon fell into a new rhythm of an earlier service in English in the town hall, followed by a Sesotho service in an old barn used as a chicken shed. One was freezing, and the other smelled awful! But with remarkable commitment, we pressed forward. At the time, I didn't realise the impact it had on me personally, and something of our original calling started to die deep within me.

Slow decline

Throughout my development and training, I was taught on many occasions about the importance of taking care of my own spiritual health and avoiding spiritual dullness. Yet, even with all the excellent teaching, our success on the ground and God continually showing himself through the miraculous, I allowed myself to slowly slip into decline without even realising its effect. Slowly but surely, I found it harder and harder to cope with the many demanding facets of our work in the mountains of the Eastern Free State. Spiritual dullness is a powerful enemy, and I soon found myself merely going through the motions. It affected every aspect of my life, leading to several poor decisions. I became less tolerant of those serving me so sacrificially, criticising the smallest of errors, and my investment in them ceased. Our personal financial situation became so difficult that I made a terrible mistake by cashing in some of our investments without sharing it with Heather, which caused her great hurt and mistrust when she found out. There were numerous excuses and considerable pressure, but we were in a slow and steady decline. Heather's mother then had several minor strokes, and so further pressure was added to our already full emotional load. Heather was in a constant state of guilt, unable to serve her family who were so many miles away. Pressure upon pressure began to weigh and wear me down.

Let's pack it in!

It was in this vulnerable and isolated state that we first voiced our thoughts of leaving the ministry and returning to our roots in Cape Town. Foolishly, I had become so isolated and didn't have a sound accountability structure in place. Pride in our success had left me relying entirely on my own ability and not seeking input from my local team or those watching over us from afar. As I withdrew, they were unaware of my decline, before it was too late. Simon Pettit had asked Ray Lowe to step back from his involvement with us for a season, and so that was a closed door, too. These were difficult days for Heather and me, and especially for the many faithful families who were serving with us.

In a moment of vulnerability and lack of leadership, I suggested to Heather that I return to business in Cape Town so that I could provide adequately for her and our family. Like Peter in the gospels, I thought "returning to fishing" was a good idea. Gone were the dreams, absent were the promises, and excluded were the friends I had so loved working with. I communicated with Simon Pettit and our local team that we would be leaving the farm in Clarens, along with our personnel, and returning to Cape Town. I had so hardened my heart that, even when Justice wept bitterly on hearing the news, I was fully convinced that we had made the right decision and that I had done my bit for God.

Chapter 21

DO YOU NOT KNOW WHO YOU ARE?

To release some of the growing pressure we were experiencing, Heather, the boys, and I headed to Cape Town to see our family and consider our future. As good as it was to reconnect with everyone, our desire to set a new course remained confusing. We were puzzled by the lack of enthusiasm for our plans within our family, and friends were also tentative in giving us their full support. On conclusion of our ten-day break, we undertook the fourteen-hour journey and returned to the farm in Clarens, no more settled than when we had left. We were no sooner home and settled on the farm, when we received a call from a friend based in Zimbabwe, Piet Dreyer.

Piet and his wife, Hettie, had pioneered some extremely fruitful work in South Africa and were now doing the same in Zimbabwe, where they had established a prosperous working farm, teaching sustainable farming methods to hundreds of Zimbabwe's rural poor. They were part of our wider church family and gave immense shape to our understanding of empowering the poor. When the call came through, we were shocked to hear that Piet was some two hours away and heading in our direction to see us. With such determination, there wasn't much we could do except to prepare for his visit.

A scolding!

From the moment of his arrival, there was no doubt Piet meant business. After Heather served refreshments, he sent the boys to play and sat with Heather and me on our front veranda. South African men are known for their forthrightness, but this was on another level! Remembering that unexpected visit, it was more like a scolding. As we sat in silence, Piet passionately persuaded us that we were making the biggest mistake of our lives, adding, "How dare you even consider leaving the ministry!" He reminded us of what we had achieved, recalled the promises made to us, and admonished me for the poor leadership of my family and the church at this time. We were silent because we knew he was right.

When I finally ventured to speak of our hopeless situation, he reached into his pocket and removed a large wad of cash, placing it before us on the coffee table. "This is for your trip to Zimbabwe next week. Pack your things, get in your car, and Hettie and I will host you for the next month. By then you'll be ready to get on with what God has called you to do." There was no discussion or entertaining of our doubts; in his mind it was clear, and we were heading to Zimbabwe for a month. I seem to remember that Piet Dreyer added a few more thoughts, said some warm goodbyes, and headed off for Pretoria that same afternoon. Shell-shocked, we made plans for the farm, informed our friends in Clarens, and packed our belongings for the month away. What incredible kindness Piet had expressed to us through his actions.

Zimbabwe

Over the years, I have had the privilege of visiting many countries, which I count as a great privilege. With all the countries I have visited, I don't think any have had the impact that Zimbabwe had on us as a family as we journeyed north. Piet and Hettie were based in Bindura, Mashonaland, which is located approximately one hour north of Harare, the capital city. For us in the Free State, South Africa, that meant an eighteen-hour journey. The first stage involved navigating through the Beitbridge border post and then finding our overnight stop at the Lion and Elephant Motel in southern Zimbabwe. We received such a warm welcome when we arrived at the motel that we could have stayed there for the month. It is evident that the growing political upheaval in Zimbabwe was having an impact, but one would not have known because of the warmth and openness with which we were received. Zimbabwe threw open her arms to warmly embrace our emotionally battered family, and already our restoration had begun.

The next morning we said our goodbyes to the dear hotel staff, and we were soon on the road again, heading north. It was a feast for the eyes! Travelling through Matabeleland, we soon reached the Motopos, which are large granite outcrops spanning a great area. As the road wound its way through these grand edifices, one could hardly take it all in, such was the beauty. Hour after hour, our journey northward was filled with the most delightful experiences, including numerous baobab trees, which made the boys laugh with excitement at these unusual "upside-down" trees. After passing through Harare and a few military checkpoints, we finally arrived in Bindura, where we were collected and escorted to Piet and Hettie Dreyer's home on the farm. The magnificence of the area is amazing, and we can remember the lines of the msasa trees displaying all their brilliance, only to be outdone by the African Flame tree with its impressive flame-coloured flowers. The farmhouse is situated alongside the Mazowe River, and one can hear the hippos in the mornings enjoying a boisterous dip in the cool river. We were given strict instructions about snakes, hippos, and crocodiles, which this area had in abundance – every move we made was supervised by Dabson, the most delightful Shona man who ran the household. Our boys were captivated by his gentleness and kindness; they had made a friend.

As we headed for bed on that first evening, completely worn out by the long journey, I heard a shriek from the bedroom to which I instantly responded. I found Heather frozen in the corner, pointing towards the wall opposite her. To my astonishment, there was the most enormous spider I have ever seen. Such was its size that my spread-out hand would not have covered it if I had tried. Zimbabwe has numerous varieties of these large arthropods, and I had no idea which one this was. I gingerly caught it and took it outside. Another shriek! My recently arrested spider was not the only one in the room, and Heather and I finally concluded that we would have to share the room with them, or I would never get any rest. If Piet had asked us to come to Zimbabwe to get our minds off our recent failures, he had already succeeded in that task before we had even made it to bed. Added to this, when we enquired about the obvious shotgun-blast marks along the walls in the passage, we were told that an aggressive Black Mumba, Africa's deadliest snake, had entered the house and had to be dealt with. Piet and Hettie's excited son, Jacques, hurriedly fetched a large glass bottle, which displayed the remains of the enormous visitor. Despite all these terrifying stories and our busy spider friends, we slept so well as it had been a long and tiring journey.

I'm not sure that any other place in the world can beat the African bushveld mornings. When we woke the following day, we were greeted by the most wonderful light and sounds of the waking bushveld. Our Zimbabwean adventure had begun.

Thrown into the deep!

Heather never missed a moment to soak in our glorious surroundings, and it was a joy to see our boys enjoying the excellent hospitality of the Dreyer family. As we said goodnight to Piet and Hettie on the second night of our visit, Piet casually said, "Steve, be ready at 4:15 a.m. and bring your Bible." I enquired as to what was happening, only to be told, "You'll see." The early start was not an issue for me, but I had clearly expressed to Piet that I wanted no preaching or teaching responsibilities during our time in Zimbabwe. His response to that was a little ambivalent, which I missed at the time.

Set up!

As I climbed into Piet's pickup truck just after 4:30 a.m. the next morning, I asked about where we were heading, only to get a very vague reply. As we bumped our way across the great farm estate, Piet quietly asked me to find a passage and get ready to bring a short encouragement. My protests were met with a large grin, and I set about finding an appropriate passage. Ten minutes later, we arrived at a large enclosure next to the barns and storage area for the farm. To my amazement, some five hundred farm workers and trainees slowly found a place to sit on the dusty earth, men to my left, women to my right. With a great cheerful response, Piet greeted everyone and then promptly explained who I was and that I would be bringing an encouragement from God's Word, after we had sung one song and prayed. I had been set up and there was now nothing I could do except to fulfil this task.

Standing before this large, attentive group, I was surprised at how easily the words flowed, and the workers' response took me aback. Many came forward in response to the message, so we had to pray over them in groups. As a result, the day started late due to the events that occurred in that compound. It was very encouraging to see God at work. As we said goodbye and sent everyone out into the fields, Piet announced that I would be speaking each morning that week and they must prepare their hearts for all God wanted to say and do.

Can you see who you are?

My protests fell on deaf ears as we drove back to the farmhouse, and all I got was a quiet chuckle from Piet. For the next three mornings, I spoke to this ever-growing group, and God began to move quite powerfully. Healings began to occur, lifting everyone's faith levels, and many responded to the gospel, putting their faith in Jesus. On the third morning, I preached a message on the Holy Spirit, and we were all taken aback by the liberty and freedom that started to manifest among these workers. It was very exciting to see. Driving back after one of the early morning meetings, Piet reached across and put a hand on my shoulder. "Do you now see who you are? Steve, we have been doing this for a very long time, and we have seen very little to no fruit among these dear people. You come; you use your gift and see what has happened! Do you know who you are? I hope you have now seen."

Looking back at that experience on the farmlands of Mashonaland, I am reminded of the time King Saul's son, Jonathan, the heir apparent, took a young, anointed brother David into a field. Jonathan stripped himself of his royal tunic, his robes, sword, and bow, placing them on David as a sign of recognition of God's call on David's life. It was a moment of deep display of humility, a moment of recognition and ownership. That's what Piet had done for me. "Now, Steve, get refreshed over the coming weeks and then go back to Clarens and be the man God called you to be." No long counselling or intense times of input. Just an older brother with a caring heart, rescuing a younger brother full of the promises of God. How the church needs more Piet Dreyers.

Piet and Hettie headed off overseas for a few weeks, leaving us to tend the farmstead. They were amazing days filled with new experiences and new friends. I spoke several times at the early morning gatherings, as well as each Sunday at the local church community, and found absolute joy as

I watched God work in and through me. As a family, we took every opportunity to experience Zimbabwe, but sadly, fuel shortages stifled any plans for long journeys. Dabson continued to make life fun and took the boys bass fishing, preparing a long bamboo pole for each boy, with a wine cork and a hook on the end of the line. Heather and I would lazily watch as the boys responded to every tug on their line that made the attached wine cork hop on the water with joy. No day passed without some form of adventure.

Zim wildlife!

We were mostly at home in the evenings, except for one night of the week when we joined a local small group gathering. With the absence of lighting, the African bushveld can be extremely dark at night, making our homeward drive quite an adventure. Once before, as we travelled along the farm track after a meeting, a tree had fallen across the track, completely blocking our route. It was only as we got closer that we realised it wasn't a tree but a massive python snake, slowly crossing the road. Once it cleared and its tail slid into the bush, we were on our way! On another dark evening, as we followed the beams of our headlights along the dusty track, a man jumped out before us, frantically waving his hands in the air. "Hippo, hippo, please let me in!" was his cry. The man clambered into the back of our car, and sure enough, the grey outline of a hippo was visible in the nearby grass. He was incredibly grateful, and our boys were buzzing with excitement at the wildness of our surroundings.

Zimbabwe is a country of vast experiences, and we are so grateful for the many opportunities Heather had to further the boys' homeschooling experience. Opportunities opened for them to learn about farming peanuts, producing peanut butter, and even taking a flight in a glider over the Zimbabwean landscape late one afternoon. All of this added significant value to the daily schooling activities at the farm homestead, which had become home.

Homeward in His strength

Our Zimbabwe adventure finally came to an end, and we prepared for our return home to Clarens, South Africa. It was truly a life-shaping time, and we felt ready to embrace the future again. The remarkable aspect for me personally was that I had begun to dream of God again. Only this time, my plan was not to do it in my own strength, but in His.

Chapter 22

A NEW COURSE

The grace of God is the most phenomenal power when embraced. Underserved and unearned, lavished upon us as followers of Jesus Christ, it transforms by its very nature. When we humbly respond to His grace pursuing us, it flows like a river in our lives. As Heather, our three boys, and I wound our way back through southern Zimbabwe, crossing the border into South Africa, we also crossed into a fresh start and a season of intentionality – a season that would be defined by grace.

Grace at work

I had witnessed this grace at work when I ministered countless times in Zimbabwe, having believed that I had nothing more to give, only to discover that there was more than I had ever imagined. But now, I needed to re-engage with a shaken church and cautious leadership in our community in Clarens. I reckoned that it would take some time for confidence in my leadership to be re-established, and so we returned, knowing that there was a great deal of ground to be re-taken if we were to see God's promises fulfilled.

Summoning all the courage we could muster, we set a new course for the church, and I committed myself to a more wholesome form of leadership, trusting I had learnt the hard lessons of relying on my own strength. God was so good, and we quickly picked up new momentum in Dihlabeng Church, although the pattern of two services, one in English and one in Sesotho, remained a challenge. As our leadership team gained new capacity, we began to dream of one church, one community, one new people. As we grappled with the challenge of facilitating this new hope for a combined community, both opportunities and difficulties came our way.

With 2001 gaining momentum, we were able to negotiate and then purchase a partially completed building that was ideal for a church gathering space. It was not a unanimous decision because, unfortunately, the building was in the commercial area of Clarens and not easily accessible for our poorer members. However, after much prayer and debate, we acquired this large unfinished warehouse. Dihlabeng Church was blessed with competent people, and we were able to design and begin the building work required to make it an acceptable facility for the church very quickly. Little did I know that this very opportunity would become the catalyst for significant disruption in the church, resulting in several key individuals leaving our community as a consequence.

Ravaged by HIV

Furthermore, the much-talked-about HIV/AIDS epidemic had begun to ravage our community, and it was no longer a concept but a destructive enemy. One and two deaths soon became tens and twenties, with numerous funerals being held each weekend. In fact, a year earlier, when I was almost at my lowest, our very gifted and talented worship leader began to show symptoms of the dreadful illness and, with an atmosphere of secrecy and non-disclosure, we finally buried him, leaving us greatly shaken. Many began to speak of this as "God's judgement on our sinfulness", and it became paramount for the leaders to lay a sound and biblical foundation of compassion and responsiveness. It's wonderful to look back and see how God shaped the hearts of our church community, allowing us to eventually become the reason for a sharp decline in this opportunistic threat.

Building work disrupted

It was late in 2001 when we were enjoying renewed fruitfulness as a church, that I visited the building site to observe the progress. We had such a dedicated team, and the office complex at the back end of the facility was taking shape. As I walked through the cavernous structure, God spoke to me. I clearly heard him say, "This is not where I want you." Due to the thorough process, I dismissed it, as surely this was to be the "forever home" of Dihlabeng Church? As hard as I tried to suppress the growing realisation that God was indeed speaking to me, the louder the discontent grew in my heart. Days became weeks, and still I couldn't overcome the feeling that we had indeed made a terrible mistake, and this was not where God wanted us. I spoke it to those I was increasingly accountable to, and they found it equally hard to counsel me in this regard. Finally, I gathered our growing leadership team and walked them through the turmoil of the heart. Sadly, my diaries do not record the details of the team's time of deliberation, but I must have convinced them, as we returned to the site and instructed our team to stop building.

Understandably, parts of the church were greatly shaken, especially knowing that we had no alternative plan, and the building process was well underway. The only thing we had to go on was "God had spoken to Steve", leaving me relatively isolated but fully supported by the leadership. I settled my heart that obedience to God can be costly but paramount, especially when God calls one to something without any explanation or detail. We held tightly to God and pressed forward, truly believing He had called us to this unusual path. This decision soon became the catalyst for several of our white South African families leaving the church and pursuing an alternative gathering. There were so many lessons for me to learn over those months, and each one played a vital part in shaping my developing leadership philosophy and style.

The hardship the church had to embrace soon became the vehicle that ushered in significant change. Working through many fractured relationships, we began to draw our two separate meetings together, hoping that one day we would truly become one. God showed His ongoing goodness to us as we began to see a fresh wave of faith being born among us. At the same time, he added key people to us. I had maintained an active link with the churches in Zimbabwe. I travelled there a few times a year, as they too were going through significant disruption due to the land invasion and political upheaval the country was facing. On one of my trips, I had the pleasure of staying with Brian and Cathy Oldrieve, pioneers of sustainable farming methods, which ultimately had a profound impact on us. They had opened their home to a long-haired, strapping young man by the name of Pete West. It was a delight to meet him, and I could see the grace of God at work in his life. As the week progressed, I became increasingly convinced that I should invite Pete to relocate to Clarens and join our church.

It was only weeks later that he arrived, having driven all the way from Bindura, Zimbabwe, in his little pickup truck. I soon discovered that Pete had the most astonishing relational gift, bringing joy, togetherness, and wholeness wherever he went. He was a relational tonic for Dihlabeng Church and soon played such an integral role in re-establishing our relational feel in the church. What a gift. Another couple whom God sovereignly sent our way, came in the most unusual circumstances – on a visit to Clarens. A local estate agent thanked me for sending Peter and Loretta Dickerson to them, as they had purchased a home. I was surprised as I had only met them briefly and had no idea that they were moving to Clarens from the Kentish town of Biggin Hill in the UK. I was staggered, but how grateful we were that God had moved their hearts to come and join us. They, along with their two girls and son-in-law, soon began to play a healing role among us, and their servant hearts were quickly to be put on full display. And so, with renewed purpose, God began to unlock our church for his intended purpose.

Chapter 23

PROMISED LAND

The statistical evidence of the impact of HIV/AIDS was proving to be more and more of a reality, both in our nation and even more significantly in our community of Clarens. The ever-increasing threat of the epidemic began to shape our thinking when the small school we had started to plug the gap of a growing lack of primary education for our town's children, saw the need to step in and provide quality education for the ever-increasing number of HIV/AIDS orphans. Under the sacrificial guidance of Margaret Grant and her team, a small, abandoned farm school building comprising two rooms, was acquired for the school, allowing us to expand our vision. The little hill-top building stood alone in a field on the outskirts of the town and proved to be an ideal location, especially when news started to filter through that the local housing was to be expanded right up to the boundary line of the school land.

Relocation

My records don't reveal who first suggested that the land on which the little school building stood would also be ideal for a large church centre. The idea took root in our hearts, and finally, we were able to approach our local government, which, surprisingly, recognised the value of allocating a section of the land to us. We were elated, and there was more than enough land to expand the school and build a three-hundred-seater facility for the church. By this time, we had sold the earlier building in the town to a business enterprise, and we had sufficient funds, supplemented by a few generous gifts, to begin developing the property.

We began to see the outworking of God's plan for us. Previously, we had only understood that we were to proceed with the previous project, but now we could see how much more effective the new site would be. For our poorer members, who made up the majority of the church, this was a much easier location to reach, and so there was great rejoicing in our church when we shared the exciting news. No sooner had the steel structure been erected and the roof sheeting applied than we moved in. The absence of walls did not deter us, and each week we could celebrate the building process in our togetherness. For the health-and-safety-minded nations, this would have been an outrageous development; however, we were so desperate to meet as one that we prepared well each week and made space for seating, ensuring the safety of each person in attendance.

Mighty men

To oversee the project, we bought two small wooden cabins, which we erected on site to serve as our office area. Dihlabeng Church was primarily a women's church in these early days, which sadly reflects much of the church culture in Africa. Our womenfolk were unequalled in zeal and commitment to the purposes of God, but rarely did we get to influence the entire family unit due to the absence of fathers. This situation was brought to our attention by Justice Mofokeng, who had by now become a driving force in our leadership team. He suggested that we observe a month of prayer and fasting to ask God for a breakthrough among the men in our community. Wonderfully and sovereignly, thirty-five men responded to the gospel a month later, and the very fabric of the church began to change. We celebrated the goodness of God!

One of those to respond to the gospel was a man by the name of Samuel Mokoena. He and his wife, like most in the Basotho culture, avidly followed traditional culture and worshipped their ancestors, something that is very difficult to withdraw from due to fear and family pressure. So convinced of the change Jesus had brought to his life, Samuel finally shared with his Zulu wife, Topsy, the news of his conversion and upcoming baptism. This came at a time of great tension when Topsy had overheard Samuel telling a neighbour about his conversion. She was horrified and spoke of all the calamity that would be poured out on their family by the ancestral spirits, and she was especially annoyed that he had not told her about his new faith. When he calmly stood his ground and testified to the reality of Jesus and his saving power, Topsy went on the attack, accusing and threatening him, even suggesting divorce, and she also decided that she would not serve him food or have a family meal together until he denounced his newfound faith. Calmly, Samuel stood his ground and loved her.

Good news to the poor

Samuel had changed, and the often closed and indifferent Basotho man became attentive, soft, and a caring husband and father. Such was the dramatic change to his very nature that it was like heaping coals on his fractious wife. Days turned to weeks, and Samuel became increasingly loving. Topsy then set about visiting Dihlabeng Church on a Sunday to check out what had made such a change in her husband. Softened by her experience in the church and Samuel's ongoing devotion to her and the family, Topsy agreed to visit Justice and Anna, who had been instrumental in Samuel's conversion, and it was there that her heart was opened. The change was as dramatic as Samuel's. Topsy's life was totally transformed by the gospel that afternoon. It certainly was good news for the poor.

From the moment Topsy began to engage in our church community, we were aware of her unusual ability, and it wasn't long before she started to play an active role in the church. Her devotion to God was unequalled, and one day I asked her if she would consider serving me as my personal assistant. We still laugh about her reply, which was, "What's a personal assistant?" We decided to work it out together, but in the process, we unlocked one of the most dynamic and beautiful gifts among us. Topsy quickly up-skilled and became the most wonderful support for all God had called me to carry, and the glue that held our ever-growing, wider influence together. Added to this, Samuel started to show such leadership grace, and it wasn't long until we began to draw them into our leadership team and, ultimately, Samuel would step into an eldership role.

An open heaven

Dihlabeng Church was on the move. There was a palpable sense of change in momentum, and, slowly but surely, the relational scars caused by the departure of several key friends began to heal. We still met in two locations on a Sunday but decided to have a week of prayer and fasting in the rather messy building, where construction was steadily proceeding. Our team carefully laid out a plan for the week, dedicating each day to one of our key priorities. Thursday was set aside for prayer and fasting for the poor in our midst and in the community. Nothing could have prepared us for what we were about to experience.

I will build my church

Each morning, about fifty of us gathered for prayer before work, delving deeper into God's presence. It was incredibly uplifting for everyone. As we started focused prayer for the poor that Thursday morning, the head teacher at our school, Margaret Grant, read a beautiful passage about the early church and their effectiveness among the poor in Jerusalem. Such was their impact that the passage in the Book of Acts of the Apostles records that "there was not a needy person among them" (Acts 4:34 ESV). Margaret highlighted this fact and then challenged us with the reason for their success, which was that they "shared their possessions". I was leading the meeting that morning, and Margaret turned to me, laughing, saying, "I don't know what we do with that!"

Our local context was extremely complex and challenging in terms of material possessions and needs. Most of our church members lived well below accepted poverty norms, while a smaller group enjoyed a comfortable life. There was a significant imbalance within our community, shaped by the effects of Apartheid with its disempowering philosophy, and local cultural drawbacks. This was not an easy journey to navigate. Our faithful gathering returned to prayer, and I quietly considered what had just been brought by Margaret. My mind drifted to my own situation: our beautifully cared-for home, my own cupboards with their neat rows of clothing, and our storerooms, packed with items we had discarded or set aside for future use. It was there that the answer lay.

We quietly gathered everyone into a huddle, and I began to instruct them, with something like this: "We all have items at home that would make a brother or sister's life just that little bit easier and lead us in the direction this Scripture displays. Items of clothing, household goods or even electronic goods. Maybe even food stuff, packed in a pantry, just in case they may be needed. I want to close off this time of prayer and ask each one here to return home and go through all your 'possessions'. Anything you have not looked at, used, or considered for the past month, please bring it to the church during the day, and tonight we will share our possessions." I instructed our small staff complement to contact every church member and explain what God had said to us at the early prayer meeting and how we believed we should respond. With an audible buzz across the room, I further instructed the poorest of the poor that they were equally responsible for playing their part, and they, too, needed to bring any unused possessions. One final instruction – no junk! Everything had to be in working order, good quality, and easily distributed. Our early morning prayer meeting concluded, and it was a joy to see the commissioned church head out to their homes.

Only your best

None of us knew how the evening gathering would play out. It could be chaos or a great blessing for many. With these thoughts occupying my mind, Heather and I headed back to our farm and began the task of identifying various items to contribute, as Father God had called us to do. We had furniture, crockery, and cutlery, all gathered and placed on the back of our pickup truck. Then it was bedding, followed by clothing. I was shocked at how quickly the rear of our vehicle filled up. Upon opening my cupboard, I saw a shoe box neatly packed at the back and remembered that I had bought a really lovely pair of shoes for future use. I already had a pair on and had planned to merely step into the new ones when I had worn out the present ones. This was a perfect opportunity! I was just about to remove my old shoes and swap them for the new ones, when I believe the Holy Spirit promptly reminded me of my instruction to the church: "Give your best!" Does God make you laugh? I chuckled and took the unopened box of new shoes, adding them to the growing pile of items for our much-anticipated evening.

When I arrived back at the church mid-afternoon, I was shocked! The large hall of our unfinished building was piled high with everything one would find in a well-stocked department store. It truly was overwhelming. At the time, we used long wooden benches for seating, and we quickly set them out in long twenty-metre rows, like one would find in a shop. We demarcated areas for clothing, furniture, household goods and foodstuffs. Slowly and carefully, the benches were filled according to their category, and it was staggering how much our small community had gathered. Even as we arranged all the goods, people were arriving with incredible bundles of items, or even just one extra cup and saucer that could be passed on. Not only was our newly built hall filled with activity and goods, but the pleasure of God was thick in the air. Fully set up, I returned to the farm and collected Heather and the boys for our evening meeting. I tried my best to share all I had seen with Heather, but nothing could have prepared us for what we were about to experience.

Beautiful and in order

Some anticipated a stampede. Others were wide-eyed and overwhelmed like me. The great hall was ready, and around the edges stood a humble, quiet crowd, window-shopping in a new way. No one was being unruly, and no one was trying to gain an advantage. It was as if everyone knew that this was a "holy moment". The rows of items awaited us like an offering before the Lord. It's hard to describe that moment fully. Looking back, we realised that not one photo was taken that night, and I've often wondered if God just wanted it to be an experience more than a captured moment.

It was time. There have been many times I have felt the inspiration of the Holy Spirit at work in ministry, but that evening was a very special one for me. I acutely felt God guide me, and we began by breaking down the gathered congregation into areas of need. We started with those who were more established and did not require additional possessions. I asked them to be "department heads" and serve those who would come in need. They gladly found a suitable area to take charge of, and quickly, every area of our "department store" was manned. Then we called the grandmothers who were caring for the grandchildren (mainly due to the HIV/AIDS epidemic) to step forward to form a queue. Followed by the single parents, the jobless and those in informal housing. Quietly and obediently, a long and orderly queue formed around the hall. Miraculously, someone had provided the largest shopping bags one could get, and each member of the queue was given one, with the instruction that they could choose one item at a time and then rejoin the queue to pass through the "shop" four times. It was glorious to watch! We then realised that several children had come alone, unaccompanied by a parent. We asked some of the adults to take them by the hand and help them choose items of need. The shopping began as if it were a time of offering, such was the order and the fun.

Watching this great spectacle unfold, I saw that Dihlabeng Church was being born anew. I had read the Book of Acts of the Apostles many times and sat in wonder at how they had achieved such unity and togetherness, knowing it would have come at a significant cost. Now, before me, it unfolded. I slowly wandered through the store and took in as much as I could. I went to the crockery section, where I happened upon an elderly grandmother who was carefully considering the most beautiful teacup. It was of excellent quality, with a delicate handle and design, and she held it up, carefully considering it. She finally decided to take it, and it was then that I realised it was part of an extensive set. I explained to her and the young person serving that she wasn't just to take the cup, but the entire crockery service, all the plates, side plates, bowls and cups and saucers – it was all hers. The look on her face is still etched in my memory, and I stepped back in awe as I realised that this is what God has done for us. He gave us his all. He held nothing back. All that He was and is became ours.

My second memory of that evening was finding a young man I knew very well standing near the shoe section. He was labouring through the variety of men's shoes to find the one he liked. I asked David what size he was looking for, and when he said ten, I gladly reached for the box I had brought to the church and encouraged him to consider it. The surprise on his face when he opened the box to find the tissue paper and wrapping all in place was a sight to behold. They were new! Brand new! He looked at me in utter amazement and slowly withdrew them from the box, placing them on his feet. They were a perfect fit. In that moment, I realised that it truly is better to give than to receive. God was changing my heart, and we would never be the same again.

With the entire shopping experience completed, we realised that we still had far too much stock. We sent everyone through, one more time, and the blessing truly overflowed. It was hard to fully appreciate all God did in us that evening in our incomplete church facility, but we knew we had experienced something very special. However, I felt God prompt me to ask if anyone had taken more than the five items they should have had in their bag. Slowly, a number stepped forward and placed extra items back on the benches. It was beautiful and pure. All the items left that night were then distributed to the poor in our town, completing our time of sharing our possessions.

One!

Our evening of distributing to each who had need changed us forever. From that moment, our two services became one, and we were never apart again. Poor and rich, black and white, employed or unemployed, young and old, Sesotho-, Afrikaans- and English-speaking, we were one. One heart, one soul, as described in Acts of the Apostles, was the early church's motto. Jesus' prayer to the Father in John 17:22 was answered among us that evening: "The glory you have given me I have given to them, that they may be one even as we are one" (ESV).

Chapter 24

GROWING FRUITFULNESS AND COMING OF AGE

In one's life, or in the life cycle of a church or church movement, there are periods of time, sometimes spanning years, that prove to be more shaping, fruitful, and profound than any other periods of time. The latter half of 2003, as well as both 2004 and 2005, were the most formative years for us as a church in Clarens. Having made substantial changes to both our leadership style and the culture of the church, these years set our trajectory to become all God had promised us – a church capable of carrying the neighbourhood, our nation, and the ends of the earth. Our dream of reaching the "ends of the earth" did not seem so unattainable as it had felt at times, and our unity in diversity became a powerful mechanism for growth and impact.

With Simon Pettit, who was based in Cape Town, taking on an increasingly fatherly apostolic lead that drew us into the nations, our togetherness across Africa began to gain significant momentum as Simon's massive vision for the church took hold in our hearts. With growing confidence among our churches in Southern Africa, many training and equipping opportunities arose, and we could see the effect on Dihlabeng Church. Very soon, God added those who had a heart for the nearby towns and villages and started to plant new churches as God led us. These were exciting days, and we would send out teams from Dihlabeng Church to strengthen these new communities in towns like Ladybrand, an hour and a half to the south. One became two, and then we seemed to multiply quite quickly.

But the true joy for me was witnessing the growth and maturity within Dihlabeng Church itself. We committed ourselves to the enormous task of completing our building, something that often seemed quite elusive. In a small, impoverished community, funds for such a large project were scarce, but this did not discourage us from pushing on. Gradually, our new church home took shape, and we met there Sunday after Sunday, regardless of the state of the construction site. With care and clarity, we introduced our first eldership team, and I recall the joy and celebration that accompanied the announcement of Justice Mofokeng, Peter Bonney, Gavin Northcote, and Sam Mokoena joining me as our future elders. As the church journeyed with us in this vision for an eldership team, many friends came in support, and in our unfinished church facility, we recognised these dear men as elders, praying over them and their families. It was a joyous occasion that brought significant maturity to our community.

Partners in the gospel

Our hand was further strengthened as God brought us together with friends from other nations. We were asked to host an "Impact Team" from the United Kingdom, a diverse team of people longing to experience the nations, and this introduced us to Mark and Jacqui Thornett, who became instant friends and continue to journey with us to this day. While overseas, Heather and I met another delightful couple from a small northern town in the United Kingdom, called Buxton. Very soon, Tim and Becky Davies travelled out to us with their young sons. We treasured these friendships, and their vast wealth of biblical knowledge significantly enhanced our understanding.

Tim and Becky's home church in Buxton was also diligently working to raise funds for a building project in their town. When they saw and heard of the struggles we were facing as we endeavoured to complete our building, they sacrificially agreed with their entire church family to give us their building funds, knowing that the favourable exchange rate would allow us to finish the church facility in Clarens. It was an act of great sacrifice, and we quickly got to work closing the last walls and rooms, fitting doors and windows. Very soon, the decorating began, with each of us contributing time and finances every step of the way. Families committed to buying the expensive lights and even small village clusters from the farms united to buy the fittings we desperately needed. It was a remarkable family project. Each step brought us closer to our goal and further strengthened our diverse community.

A constant battle

However, amid this period of significant progress, the challenges of the growing HIV/AIDS epidemic seemed to haunt us persistently. Weekends were rarely free of funerals, and we lost some dear friends. Cloaked in secrecy and non-disclosure, the debilitating disease appeared to have the upper hand. Peter and Loretta Dickerson had purchased a handy double-cab pickup truck, which they freely used to assist with the building project. However, the requests for help in transporting desperately sick individuals to the provincial hospital seemed to increase steadily. On one occasion, they took a very weak lady to a regional hospital only to find the waiting room overcrowded and the hospital hopelessly understaffed. They asked staff when the doctor might assist the lady they had brought, only to hear of the overwhelming workload on all the medical personnel; it was a somewhat hopeless situation. They returned from that hospital visit rather dejected, with many questions left unanswered.

People of hope

The reality was that our nation faced one of the world's most significant challenges, as it was predicted that South Africa would have more than five and a half million sufferers, with at least twenty per cent of the fifteen- to forty-year-olds infected by the disease. These figures were terrifying, and it meant we could expect more than six hundred sufferers at any one time in our small town. Something had to be done, so we gathered like-minded people and set about finding solutions. During the meeting, Loretta referenced the term "people of hope", and instantly, a ministry called People of Hope was born. Offering home-based care, the growing team, under Loretta's guidance, soon had more than three hundred and fifty clients, and the extraordinary task of serving and educating the community began.

Looking back at those small beginnings facing such a giant as HIV/AIDS, it's heart-warming to recognise that this group of dedicated people led by Lorretta and Peter, followed by Topsy Mokoena with her faithful team, fought one of our greatest battles, only to overcome it when, over a six-year period, the number of clients dropped from hundreds at any one time to less than twenty. It's not often a project like this closes due to its own success, but that's the outcome of this remarkable initiative. They truly became "people of hope".

Seeing the heart

It was during these exciting and challenging days that I received the most surprising email from Simon Pettit. The main message of the email was an invitation to join a small team of men with emerging apostolic gifts to serve our expanding work in Southern Africa. He carefully outlined the details of what it would involve and asked me to confirm my participation through email. The request completely took me aback, as I had been focusing on building well in Dihlabeng Church, and I was especially surprised given the difficult times we had recently experienced and our recent desire to leave the ministry. It was a period of rediscovering my vision and values, and I had soberly acknowledged that my past failures would prevent me from taking on broader leadership roles. I accepted Simon's invitation to join this small team, but I also expressed the need to meet with him, explaining that I was struggling to connect my recent difficulties with his generous offer.

When the team gathered for the first time in Johannesburg, I took the opportunity to sit with Simon and discuss my recent difficult journey. I told him that I was extremely humbled by his reaching out to me after the way I had so poorly managed myself. His response was one of the most shaping personal lessons I have ever learned, hence my desire to include it in this narrative. After listening to my account of the recent past, he firmly replied, "You have certainly been quite foolish to say the least, but God has shown me your heart and that's what I'm believing in." I was humbled by that time, realising that anyone would believe in me to that extent and take such a risk on my behalf. I remember asking God, "I'm not sure what gift that is, maybe the gift of discernment, but whatever it is, I ask that you give me the ability to believe in a man by understanding his heart." That brief conversation is possibly the start of a journey for me to truly understand what it means for one man to devote himself to another's success. What a lesson.

A mighty oak falls

God's promises of a bright and glorious future for us as a church continued to guide us, and the community prospered in every way. Growth was steady, and many key couples joined the fresh vision we faithfully carried. In October 2004, God gave me a very clear vision of "a mighty wave" about to strike us. In the vision, God showed me the destructive power of this tsunami and how many would lose their way as a result. With it came the instruction to warn those we worked with. Not knowing what to do with what God had revealed, I spoke to Simon and shared the horrific nature of what was soon to happen.

A few weeks later, on 26th December 2004, a massive tsunami struck the Far East, with devastating results. Many, many lost their lives as it swept across islands with great destructive power. As the world rallied to serve these nations, I was reminded of this vision that had come, but I never fully understood how it related to us as well. Some two weeks later, on 15th January 2005, Heather and I were getting ourselves ready for a quiet Saturday on the farm. It was a beautiful day, as only this area can produce, and we were going to make the most of it. However, at around 9 a.m. that morning, our landline phone rang and I was surprised to hear the voice of our dear friend, Jeff Kidwell. After greeting me warmly as he always did, he went on to share that Simon Pettit had passed away a few hours earlier.

If ever there was a life that exemplified devotion to Christ, it was Simon's. Alongside his wonderful wife, Lindsay, they had sacrificed so much for God and for us. It was true that a mighty tsunami had struck us, disrupting the continuity of our work across nations. Soon after this news broke, a prophetic word was given, speaking of Simon as a "mighty oak". The word declared that a mighty oak had fallen, and from the space it had occupied, many saplings would grow and rise. It is now our time to rise and be fruitful.

Chapter 25

SONS IN THE HOUSEHOLD

Laying the foundations for any new building is often the most unglamorous task in a construction project. Foundations are typically hidden underground and are not celebrated with much fanfare, as people wait for the real building to emerge. However, foundations are undoubtedly the most essential part of any project, as they establish the tone for the entire structure. For three years, we focused on the spiritual foundations of Dihlabeng Church, but as we moved further into 2004 and 2005, it seemed as though the church began to emerge above ground level. It was a joy to see.

Many years earlier, God had placed a deep desire on my heart to raise many sons and daughters within our household. In the story of Abraham found in the Book of Genesis, there comes a point when his years of wandering seem to be at an end, and he settles in the land that God had promised. There, he becomes very deliberate about raising sons in his household; indeed, three hundred and eighteen are mentioned in that passage of Scripture. While contemplating the important task before me, I was also influenced by Paul's reference to himself as a "master builder". Having made many "building" mistakes, I longed to become a "master builder" of the church, the people of God

– constructing something beautiful and majestic, lasting enough to be passed down to future generations. In fact, this desire became central to my prayer life, and I pursued it passionately. With these guiding thoughts in my heart, we decided to organise a leadership conference called Master Builders, primarily focused on raising sons and daughters within our household.

With a meagre budget of R40,000 (approximately $2,000), we hosted eighty-plus key leaders and birthed what was to become an annual event of great significance. For ten years, this event flourished and played a significant role in raising many sons and daughters. It was an exciting adventure planning our first Master Builders, knowing it marked the beginning of a great adventurous journey. We designed a logo and quickly set about making a large banner for the stage. We had just about settled on a sizable banner of some three or four metres in length, when one of our passionate and prophetic members, Martie du Plessis, vehemently objected, saying that our vision was far too small! She promptly took over the task and produced a banner nine metres in length, smiling her way through the task. "God's about a great work," she said, "therefore we need to put it on display!" Such was the expectation of our very first Master Builders and I was thrilled by this passionate response.

Here I am, send me

The first gathering was a great success, and at no point did we "despise the day of small beginnings". I still remember urging everyone with Isaiah's words, "Here am I, send me!"

calling on our expanding leadership community to be those ready to embrace our worldwide vision and call. Around dinner tables, we enjoyed not only the delicious food but also met an increasingly larger number of people from other towns and cities. Our influence began to expand. A family was being formed and we celebrated every moment of it. It was early days, but we started to see sons and daughters emerge from within our ranks.

One born in the household

Mme Mamotiisetsi Mokoena, often called Mme Emily at our church, had been a dedicated member of Dihlabeng Church for many years, participating as much as she could. Life required her to work long and tiring hours at a local Clarens restaurant at night and in some local homes during the day. Mme Mamotiisetsi always brought a vibrant and impactful presence to meetings at Dihlabeng Church. When she felt something was not right, she would boldly confront me with her big smile and passionately argue her case; nothing could stop her. We loved her, and she served faithfully, always asking for prayer for her children. Mme Mamotiisetsi had seven children with her husband, a local builder in Clarens. Life was tough for any black family finding their way during and after Apartheid. Still, Mamotiisetsi did all she could to inspire her family not to be held back by the past, but to look to Jesus, who held their future. When she was not working or at church, she would gather a few friends at her home, especially her dear friend Mme Mamorena, and they would pray for their families and the church. Her faith was inspiring, and her determination was endless.

Having had twins, Mme Mamotiisetsi's fourth child was a little boy aptly named Fusi. In the culture, a child born after twins is almost always named Fusi, "the one who follows twins". Heather and I first met Fusi when he was in his early twenties and working at our local restaurant to earn money to support his university studies. It wasn't an easy life studying and travelling to and from university, but Fusi was always full of joy, smiled incessantly, and carried out his duties at The Street Café with great diligence. We loved to be served by him whenever we ate at that restaurant, and our three young boys were especially captivated by this young, kind man who interacted so comfortably with them. His life, like that of most young men in rural South Africa, had been shaped by village life, which meant everyone had to play their part. For Fusi, this required attending school in the mornings, heading home to feed cattle and care for chickens, and then spending a few hours tending their very productive vegetable plot. Life was full for this young man. Fusi loved his sport, enjoying his football, and when not playing sport, he would be required to help his father, Ntate Nchabane, with building contracts in the town. Being a busy young man, Fusi was not overly interested in church. Still, his mother, Mamotiisetsi, never missed an opportunity to call on him and his siblings to faithfully follow Jesus in life. Fusi's mother had one big desire – she wanted to see all her children surrender their lives to Jesus before she died. For her, that was her life's mission.

In 2004, the Christian world was abuzz with news of Mel Gibson's film, *The Passion of the Christ*. At that time, our nearby town of Bethlehem had a small cinema, and we were excited to hear that they would be screening *The Passion of the Christ*. Our leadership team discussed the movie, and eventually we decided to take the entire church to Bethlehem for the screening. For most, it was to be their very first visit to a cinema, making it a significant event for our church. I coordinated with the theatre owners, who were fellow believers, to organise a special viewing, and we hired out the entire theatre.

Mme Mamotiisetsi seized a moment she couldn't miss. She arranged for all her older children to attend, and they joined our excited church family as we boarded a bus for the thirty-minute journey to Bethlehem. I need not elaborate on the harrowing nature of this film for those who've seen it, but for Mme Mamotiisetsi, it had the intended effect on her children. Both Fusi and his elder brother, Victor, attended that screening and then wrestled with what they had seen. What had previously been mere words now came to life, capturing their minds. For a whole month, Fusi reflected on and absorbed what he had seen. When he returned to Clarens from university for a weekend shift at the restaurant, he visited his mother only to find her praying fervently with her friend Mme Mamorena. During that prayer, Mme Mamotiisetsi beckoned Fusi to sit beside her and shared the gospel of Jesus with him. Fusi was prepared. In that tender moment between mother and son, Fusi quietly prayed and surrendered his life to Jesus. It was a humble but profound conversion. It was only a few weeks later that he heard from his brother Victor that he had also given his life to Christ that same day. Mme Mamotiisetsi's faith was rewarded.

We were overjoyed upon hearing the news the following week, and I was personally delighted when both Fusi and Victor began attending Dihlabeng Church. They were so bright and full of energy, which contributed to the overall enthusiasm of the church. Two months later, I had the honour of baptising them in our river, alongside more than thirty others.

The big ask

As we reached the end of the year and I realised that Fusi would soon complete his university course, I sat with him to discuss the future. From the earliest days, it was clear that God's hand was upon this young man in his twenties. His brilliant mind constantly questioned profound concepts, and he had an amazing ability to devour books and remember most of what he read. I was also reminded of what God had said many years earlier: "Fusi will be one of your leaders." Now, seven years later, we sat together considering what lay ahead. Sadly, I discovered I was not the only one pursuing Fusi. Another influential businessman from Johannesburg had also made a proposal, promising a great career, a steady income, a company car, and a very bright future in senior management. I must admit, my heart sank when I heard the details. We had no funds; God controlled the future, and my promises were limited. At the time, we only had R600 ($50) per month to support him – barely enough for his living expenses, let alone a car. I loved this young man. After considering all options, we agreed that Fusi would go away to seek the Lord, then give me his decision the following week.

A few days later, he asked to speak to me about his future, and I had deliberately guarded my heart and prepared for the news that he would be leaving for Johannesburg early the following year. Who wouldn't do that with everything on offer? Fusi would. Having prayed it through, Fusi confirmed that God indeed wanted him to dedicate himself to His purposes and start the journey by committing himself to me and Dihlabeng Church. I tried my best to hide my surprise, but I was overjoyed. Fusi joined eight other young people on our year of training, and it was clear to see that he was in the right place – God had big plans for him.

Over the months, I gradually asked him to take on responsibilities, and in every task, he demonstrated the great capacity God entrusted to him. He and I still laugh about the time I lost my voice at our Master Builders conference, and just before the meeting, I gave Fusi the responsibility of leading the gathering. With limited time to prepare and many questions, he stepped up, and his leadership grace was evident before everyone. I cannot recall the exact occasion, but I remember being moved by God in a way similar to how Simon Pettit had been many years earlier. I placed both hands on Fusi's chest and prayed an apostolic anointing over him. It was so clear, even in those early stages of his development, that God had called him to this broader role of being apostolic, "a sent one". With that in mind, I asked him to relocate to our new church plant in Maseru, Lesotho, where he served on the developing team for a season, living in some of the most challenging circumstances. That first commission led to greater things when I suggested that Fusi serve in one of our churches in the United Kingdom. He grasped the opportunity and moved to Worthing in the south of England, where he was enjoyed and recognised for the emerging gift within him.

Praise God for praying mothers. It was only after Fusi's mother's death that the children found Mme Mamotiisetsi's small prayer and fasting booklet, which was given to each member at Dihlabeng Church during a week of prayer and fasting. Inside, they discovered each of their names and notes detailing their mother's wishes for their lives. Mission accomplished. Rest in peace, Mme Mamotiisetsi.

Sons and daughters

Fusi was one of many we raised over those years, but his story is an important part of our wider church family's narrative as it unfolds. Never did I believe that one day, this sincere young man would grow in his gift, experience, and capacity, to take over from me and lead the global movement I would later birth. Our deliberate effort in nurturing our sons and daughters played a vital role in our future success, and I remain thankful to God for the talented and humble children born into our household. Sadly, there are too many to mention here, but each one is cherished. We can now celebrate them and watch as they continue to achieve remarkable things across the nations to this day.

Chapter 26

IT WAS RAW, BUT EFFECTIVE

The shock on my face must have been clear to the lady standing before me, because she repeated her request a second time. "Please help me, I want to give birth to a snake that lives inside me." We were at the front of our church building, among many who had come forward for prayer at our 2007 "Come to the River" conference. It was noisy and fully booked. Our church was growing steadily, along with our influence in the towns and villages across our region. Now, everyone was packed inside our building, and it was busy. Standing before me was a woman of about thirty years or more with this most unusual request. She looked very distressed, and I could see she was in severe pain.

I called one of my fellow Basotho leaders and asked him to help me understand what was happening. After ten years of ministering across rural Africa, I had seen many strange things, but this one was most unusual. She found it easier to converse in Sesotho, and I waited patiently for the translation. Finally, I was told that she was a witch doctor from one of our nearby towns where we had recently established a church, and one of the church members had shared the gospel with her. She had accepted Jesus as Lord and Saviour. She told us that not many visited her because everyone knew of her power and that she lived with this enormous snake. Even so, as a witch doctor, many came to her knowing she could achieve incredible things. Now she wanted this snake to come out. To fully understand what we were dealing with, I asked her a few questions, and she explained that the snake lives inside her. Undeniably, she appeared to be at least six months pregnant.

I contacted Topsy Mokoena, Mathapelo Mokoena, and Lorretta Dickerson to explain the situation. Their disbelief was apparent, but I gave them instructions on how we needed to proceed. As directed, they took this dear woman to the ladies' toilet area and began praying over her, rebuking the work of the devil in her life. Jesus was spoken of as the one who came to undo the works of the devil, and then He empowers His church to do the same. Now, here we were, ministering to someone in great need. My capable team of women stayed with her for a time as she writhed in pain and discomfort. Finally, with the door of the toilet cubicle open, she entered and, like a woman in labour, proceeded to give birth to something indescribable. Mme Topsy told me that she and the women were brave but terrified, fearing they might face this demon-snake. Thankfully, this was not the case, and there was much relief.

While this continued behind closed doors, I ministered to those in need at the front of our church. During this time, my attention was interrupted by a very presentable and shiny-faced lady. She had been tapping me on the shoulder for a while, and when I finished praying, I turned to assist her. Not recognising her, I asked what I could pray for, and she smiled, saying, "No, I'm the lady who had the snake!" Her appearance was so transformed that I would never have believed it was the same person. She radiated as if brand new. The pregnant-looking stomach was gone, the distress had vanished, and now she had the beautiful aura of a restored child. Behind her stood my faithful team of ladies, smiling, relieved, and somewhat overwhelmed. This incident reminded us all of the great task to stay relevant in the world. Sadly, the modern church can often overlook its role and power to transform lives, regardless of how dark they may be. In these uplifting days of growth through Dihlabeng Church and the churches we were now gathering, the supernatural was a constant presence, which we desperately needed in such broken communities. As with this lady, we were also making significant progress in impacting the towns and villages of our region.

Ask me for the nations

I'm sure, like me, many must have questioned God's wisdom in placing Dihlabeng Church and its world-changing vision in such a small rural town in South Africa. So much was against us: a four-hour travel by road to any airport, limited internet accessibility, and the constant poverty that surrounded us. It had the power to disqualify us from being truly significant in God's purposes. However, the grace evident in this simple church community was remarkable. In fact, the impact of the church was so profound across our region that we soon heard that the government of our province had recently changed the region's name. Moving away from the Apartheid-link names, they introduced the new name, "Dihlabeng". When the process of finding a new name began, someone whose work had greatly impacted ours suggested that we consider our church's name, as we were influencing education, healthcare, poverty alleviation, and creating job opportunities. And so, with much joy, we watched as the road signs and location signs began to change, cherishing the fact that we now lived in the Dihlabeng region.

With our growing confidence, we placed a nine-metre printed banner across the front of our church that quoted Psalm 2, "Ask me for the nations!" With this large request before us, we never missed an opportunity to ask God for the nations of the world. As our Master Builder's conference continued to grow and gain momentum, so the nations started to arrive in significant numbers, and we celebrated God's faithfulness. With our growing stature as a cluster of churches, I received an invitation to join an international group of some forty leaders from across our wider Newfrontiers family in the United Kingdom. Each one invited was carrying responsibility for more than their local church, and it was accepted that this showed what the Bible recognises as an emerging apostolic gift. Found in the likes of those who pioneered churches in the Bible, we began a journey to understand how these God-given people-gifts work, how they serve the church, and how we could multiply their effectiveness across the nations. Twice a year, I began travelling to the United Kingdom, where people like Terry Virgo, David Holden, and David Devenish would bring the most inspiring biblical teaching.

With our growing influence as a family of churches across the nations, we have discovered a clear correlation between the recognition and release of these pioneering people-gifts detailed in Scripture, and the birth of new churches. Being in the room with all these fellow church leaders of great capacity was breath-taking, and even though I'm not sure

I contributed much to the debate, they were some of the most formative years of my ministry. Furthermore, they were a testimony to Terry Virgo and his team, as they filled a room with leaders of great ability and capacity. We owe that generation an immense debt.

Generational blessings

In this season of great fruitfulness and advance as a church, God was ever so faithful in providing for and watching over us as a family. Life on the farm was often complicated and disheartening, especially when we faced an attack one night. However, God never left us alone. Heather had now home-schooled our three boys for ten years, and her diligence was paying off. Farm life for our family was rich in many ways, and we saw the evidence in our boys, who had a broad, family-oriented education. However, it became clear that, as our eldest son, Cameron, reached his final two years of school, Heather's level of expertise began to show its limits, and we had to find an alternative plan to lessen the load on her. The growing pressure of carrying their education was becoming a great weight, especially with her longing and determination to see the boys enter university after their school years. After conducting extensive investigations, we decided to send the two older boys to a small private school located about an hour and a half away from Clarens.

At times, Heather had felt that her education of the boys had been sorely lacking, but as their confidence grew in their new school environment, it was very clear that they were more than equipped and capable. They soon settled in and made many new friends. At the end of Cameron's first year at the school, we were invited to the school's year-end prize-giving and the announcement of the following year's student leaders. Sadly, I was not feeling well and eventually decided not to go with Heather, thinking that I would give everyone a rather bad dose of the flu, so I climbed into bed.

Later that night, as Heather made her way back home after the evening at the school, she called me, and I could hear tears of joy. She explained that all the teaching staff and students have the annual responsibility of choosing the head boy and girl of the school, and they had unanimously chosen Cameron for the role of head boy the following year. In the few short months Cameron was at the school, he had prospered and was rewarded for both his academic achievements and character. The fact that Heather was there alone to witness this wonderful recognition of her homeschooled eldest son was such a reward for her sacrifice in moving to a church plant, establishing a homeschool even when it was very frowned upon in our nation, and having to believe God that He would provide all she needed at every stage. This was especially dear to me; she deserved every accolade, as her sacrifice had allowed us to impact the nations.

Often in the advance of the church, we overlook the great cost families pay and how God provides so amazingly in every respect. What a faithful God. Not only did Cameron go on to play a key role at school, but over the years, all three boys – Cameron, Richard, and Adam – have achieved outstanding qualifications and prospered in life. To this day, they watch over each other with great care and much humour, and they never miss an opportunity to remind their father and mother of some of the unusual things we got up to. Bravo, Heather, pioneering mother and teacher of note!

Chapter 27

REMEMBERING THE POOR

The Newfrontiers family of churches had grown to become a movement of thousands of churches by 2008. When gathered, you would hear so many different languages spoken, and it was staggering to see the movement's breadth. Each year, leaders from around the world gather in Brighton for a time of input and togetherness, hosted by Terry Virgo. These were rich times that held us together and empowered us for when we would return home to our diverse contexts. Ten years earlier in 1998, Simon Pettit spoke at one of the main sessions on the title "Remember the Poor". Such was the insight of his teaching that it shifted the very fabric of who we were, and a new focus was born. Before Simon's untimely death, he championed this great call on our churches, ensuring that the movement of churches maintained this biblical mandate.

Approximately two years after Simon's death, I was asked to lead a task team of selected individuals who would ensure that we continued to remember the poor. David Devenish had included me in another task team focused on ministering in new nations, and I was in awe, given all the complexities involved. Those times in his team were memorable and formative, and he kindly guided me into this new task, helping to shape our journey. From small beginnings, our diverse team of men and women from different nations debated, planned, prayed, and sought God for answers to many questions related to the poor. One of the things we always did was spend considerable time in prayer, which served us very well. It was during one of these prayer sessions that I felt led to bring a prophetic word to the group. In it, was this clear statement.

> "I have not given you the poor as a project, says the Lord, but as co-equal partners in the gospel."

As we reflected on this word, we realised that we often relate to the poor through ministries or projects, but now God was calling us to recognise their value in advancing the gospel. Additionally, we recognised that this was to be achieved by embracing the poor. It was a significant shift for me, and from that moment on, this understanding transformed our entire approach. When Simon Pettit first championed the cause of the poor among us in Newfrontiers, a survey was conducted to determine how many churches had active ministries among the poor. At that time, it was just over sixty ministries worldwide. Our newly formed task team set out to champion this mandate with Simon Pettit's message still fresh in our hearts, and we were encouraged by the gradual growth in momentum across the globe.

One of the methods we used to bring churches up to speed on this biblical mandate was to hold three-day events in various nations around the world. This took us to countries like India and Malaysia, and we also hosted an event for our Russian-speaking family in my hometown of Clarens, South Africa. These were precious moments, and we celebrated their fruitfulness. One of the unexpected benefits was the growth of relationships across the world. On one occasion in South Africa, I had dinner with a Russian leader who was approximately the same age as me. Through an interpreter, we shared stories about our lives and how our two very different contexts shaped us.

During the conversation, he mentioned that he had passed Cape Town in a frigate on his way to Angola in West Africa. This caught my attention, and I told him that I had been conscripted to serve in our military in Angola in 1978. He smiled knowingly and said to me that he was there at the same time, but we were on opposing sides! We were shocked to discover, through further conversation, that we were based very near to each other in southern Angola. The gospel had transformed both of our lives, and now we sat together, no longer enemies but brothers in Christ. We laughed together as we considered this unlikely outcome. The gospel truly is a vehicle for peace.

From the sixty-plus ministries across the Newfrontiers family of churches in the early years, we were able to identify over six hundred by ten years later. It was a very shaping and impactful time.

The master builder at Master Builders

If you've ever seen the flight path of an airliner, you will know that it travels in a straight line and then often makes sharp course adjustments for its destination. I believe that these sudden and defining changes in course are called "way points". 2008 was a "way point" for Dihlabeng and our growing cluster of churches, which now included two communities in the United Kingdom. Once again, it was centred around our Master Builders conference in Clarens, which it seemed God was using powerfully. What began as a small leaders gathering was now a robust and well-attended gathering, with many travelling in from across the nations.

While in the United Kingdom, I had the pleasure of having dinner with Terry Virgo, the leader of our Newfrontiers global movement, which was always a joy. Newfrontiers was by now a substantial family spanning many nations, but Terry's interest in the detail of what God was doing through us in seemingly insignificant places was inspirational. Over the years of hosting the Master Builders conference, I had never dreamed of inviting him and his wife, Wendy, to be with us. His international preaching and teaching ministry was in great demand, and Master Builders was a relatively small rural African gathering. Over dinner, Terry asked me if I would consider inviting him to Master Builders. I was significantly taken aback as I had shelved the idea of having him in Clarens, thinking we were too insignificant. With much joy, I gratefully accepted, and Terry and Wendy Virgo joined us for the 2008 Master Builders conference.

My notes of the event record the excellent foundation of building a church family that he brought to us, emphasising the role of leadership and the local church. Having Terry with us added a new weight of expectation and self-belief, and our churches continued to blossom. While debriefing after the conference, Terry and Wendy confirmed that they would return in 2009 for the next Master Builders conference. Life seemed to pick up pace after this, and we had much to celebrate in all we were doing.

Winds of change

Late in 2008, I received an email from Julian Adams, a respected prophet among the churches. We shared a history at The Bay Community Church and developed a growing friendship, which I thoroughly enjoyed. Julian detailed how God had dropped me into his heart, and a long and insightful prophetic word followed. It spoke of a move onto the international stage where God would give me influence over leaders and nations. It was what I would call a "big word" and, although exciting, didn't quite fit into my present framework of ministry. However, I held onto it and waited for God to provide more insight.

Furthermore, while researching the details of this period I came across an interesting word that God gave me. During a time of worship, God had shown me an enormous, fully grown tree, lifting its roots from the soil, like a lady would gather her skirt to run. With its roots clearly lifted, the tree began to run with purpose. It was an unusual picture, but one I quietly considered. Where were we about to run to?

Chapter 28

I'LL GO!

The drive from O.R. Tambo International Airport in Johannesburg to our farm in the Eastern Free State town of Clarens is approximately four hours. The long, straight highway can be relatively uneventful at times, but if one takes the time to observe, there are some beautiful sights along the way. The freeway takes you through what is called the "breadbasket of South Africa", because it produces so much of our nation's crops, and so one will see miles of cultivated fields on either side of the road. Some forty-five minutes from the airport, one passes a huge fenced-off farm that goes on for many miles, and if you look carefully, you may see Sable Antelope, Lechwe and multiple Blesbok in the fields. The Sable Antelope is always my favourite to spot as it stands so proudly with its long, majestic, rear-facing curved horns, a tangible symbol of great strength and power. It is a route that those of us living in Clarens are very familiar with, as we have all travelled it frequently to collect friends and family from the airport. It's an excellent time to catch up on all the news, even though it can be pretty tiring at times.

It was March 2009, and the time for the Master Builders conference had arrived once again. We were near capacity in terms of bookings, and our administration team worked frantically to finalise all the last details. I had travelled to Johannesburg to collect Terry Virgo, our main speaker, and it was a privilege to have him with us once again. We were full of expectation; the work was prospering, and a real strength was developing among us as a growing cluster of churches. We had asked Terry to lay a fresh foundation of grace in our churches, and we had agreed that he would do it over three main sessions. We had prepared everyone, and so the stage was set for what we believed would be a remarkable few days together. We were also privileged to have Julian Adams join us as a recognised prophetic voice, and we knew he would add significant weight to Terry's Bible teaching ministry.

As Terry and I journeyed together towards Clarens, we chatted about all that had been happening across our family of churches and snippets of news about our families. It was always a joy to have these times, even though the eleven-hour overnight flight was taking its toll on Terry. One of the topics we discussed was our church in Dubai, located in the Middle East. Terry shared how the couple leading had done such an impressive job of gathering a fragile situation and turning it into something quite beautiful. However, he shared, they now felt they had fulfilled their two-year commitment to the church and would be leaving in November, just eight months away. He shared how challenging this was, as the church had at last reached a measure of maturity and strength after many turbulent years.

As I listened to Terry share his heart about Dubai, a strange and unexpected thing happened: from deep within me, the words, "I'll go!" came. Gripping the wheel of the car tightly,

I questioned myself and where the words had come from and slowly turned to gauge Terry's reaction. Terry's long night on the plane had won, and he had dropped off to sleep, leaning against the window. I had no idea whether he had heard my statement, and I was left to ponder my thoughts alone. Go to Dubai? Me? It was the strangest situation, and an enormous conflict raged within my heart.

No more big moves

The work in Dihlabeng Church and our wider region was going extraordinarily well at the time. After years of uncertainty and conflict, we had laid a solid foundation and were thriving. Our work among the poor was demonstrating signs of a significant impact in the community, and our school continued to grow, gathering the most vulnerable children in our town. Peter and Jo West, along with their three boys, had moved and settled in the north-eastern area of Lesotho, where they were playing a fantastic role in planting churches and impacting the socio-economic structures through sustainable farming practices. We had added several excellent people to our leadership team, and we were in one heart and mind. David and Cynthia Turner's computer literacy and English skills training programme had unlocked the talents in so many, enabling them to find employment or start small businesses. There was so much to celebrate.

A few weeks prior to my journey with Terry, Heather and I had sat on our front *stoep* and unpacked all we had experienced over the past few years and how the goodness of God had relentlessly pursued us. It was a wonderful time of remembering both the challenges and celebrating the advances we had seen. We had commented on what a happy place our local Dihlabeng Church was in and how many significant young people we had. It hadn't been a journey without pressure or disappointments, but the good far outweighed any struggles we may have faced. In this moment of sober assessment, Heather quietly but firmly stated that she could never do another big move again. The move from Cape Town, with its family and familiarity, had been incredibly costly for her, and she was grateful to have now settled in such a beautiful place. Our boys were in a good place, and we were at last finding our feet financially. There were no plans to move, and I had no desire to look for more outside of what we were doing, so I didn't really comment or even feel the need to.

Now, on this motorway journey from Johannesburg, God had arrested me, and I had just offered to move to the Middle East. I was relieved to discover, as we pulled into a refreshment station, that Terry had not heard my offer to be the one to move to Dubai and relieve the couple leaving in November. Although I sighed with relief, I knew God was working in my heart. Dubai?

Master Builders 2009

The Master Builders weekend was all we hoped it would be. Liberty, freedom, and family, all underpinned by the Word of God. Terry Virgo took us on a journey of discovery, wonderfully explaining the true meaning of grace, bringing freedom from wrong thinking, which had been a constant among us. For many, coming from a fear-based ancestral background, the understanding of God's undeserved favour was astonishing, and they grasped it with all they had. At times, one could hear people physically gasp at the truth of this wonderful gospel, realising it was the grace of God that had brought them this far, not their own hard work. In this atmosphere of great appreciation and truth, God encountered almost everyone in the room. This was a very special and rich time.

'All give as a family'

On Saturday night, the third evening of Master Builders, we prepared for our customary offering, which would be used for various initiatives. Everyone had been prepped before coming, and it was always a high point of Master Builders. The previous year, we had asked Terry Virgo where the offering should go, and he had suggested the Philippines, where a small church in Manila was doing its best to buy a church facility. There was such joy in that act of giving to the Philippines that we approached the offering with great expectation. I was leading the meeting that evening, and as I prepared to bring our worship time to a close and take up the offering, I felt God prompt me to "all give as a family". The words resonated within me, and I struggled to understand what that meant. As I allowed things to go on a bit longer so that I could get myself ready, I felt God reminding me that every time we attended a church gathering, I used to ensure that every member of our family had something to give. There we go, I understood!

I explained to the congregation what God had said, and then I asked everyone who had no offering to raise a hand.

This was not a normal thing to do, but slowly, some fifty hands were raised. I asked them to keep their hands in the air, and then I instructed everyone else to take some of what they had for the offering and share it with one of those with their hands in the air. It was fun! The noise, the laughter and the outrageous act of sharing unlocked something very special. With our lively worship setting the tone, people streamed forward carrying their special gifts. This was no ordinary event; there was joy and togetherness in this act of worship that we had not seen before. It seemed to go on and on as people emptied their wallets and purses and returned to the baskets at the front.

When the room had finally got some order, I felt I should pray a prayer of thanks over every coin or note that had been given. For me, it felt as if we had experienced a "holy moment" and I wanted to give thanks to God, celebrating the incredible privilege of giving. I asked everyone to be still and to raise their hands in humble submission. In this wonderful posture, we stood before God. It was still a great contrast to a few minutes earlier. Terry Virgo was just about to bring his third and final message on the theme of grace, but we were in no hurry. We were before God.

Holy wave of His presence

I lifted my hands high over the hundreds of people before me and began to give thanks for what we had just done and for the joy of being a part of it. I was no sooner into my prayer when a wave of God's presence swept from the back of our church facility, right up to the front. Like a Mexican wave at a sporting event, it rolled through the congregation, and people fell where they stood, some crying with joy, others wailing under the weight of God's presence. It was chaos, something I had never seen on this magnitude before.

With the growing crescendo of worship in the room, I had no way of calling for order. Our people were experiencing God, and He filled the room. I slowly made my way over prostrate people on the carpet and went to Terry in the front row. I explained to him that I didn't know what to do as he was meant to be preaching by this time. He laughed joyfully and said, "God's here, you don't need to do anything!"

As the Holy Spirit continued to work among our people, I quietly moved to the side of the platform and sat down, hands out. I needed to talk to God. I remember asking God what was going on, what had happened in the car, and what was going on in my heart. Quietly, God spoke to me deeply in my heart. "This is me. I want you and Heather to go to Dubai." As I was considering God's words, Julian Adams took the platform and prophesied, word for word, the prophetic message he had sent me in December via email. I knew that word so well, and now, right here, it came powerfully for everyone to hear.

God wanted us in Dubai.

Chapter 29

I CAN DO THAT!

The gospels record that Mary Magdalene and the other women ran back to the apostles to report that they had seen and spoken to Jesus after the resurrection. It records that they were "afraid but full of joy", such a strange combination of emotions. That best described my state of mind as Master Builders ended. I drove Terry back to the airport, celebrating all the way, but never mentioned a word to him about what was happening in my heart, as I needed to talk to Heather. With her words, "I could never do another big move again," ringing in my ears, I couldn't mention a word to anyone until we had considered this together before God. I told God that if He were indeed calling us to Dubai, He would have to persuade Heather, I was not going to do any arm-twisting.

When peace and quiet returned to the farm, I decided to take a few days to seek the Lord. I was carrying a lot in my heart, and my mind was buzzing with thoughts of everything that lay ahead. Heather quickly picked up on the fact that something was happening, although she said nothing. She told me later that she wondered what it could be – another move? In her quirky way, she decided to practise the word "No!" She concluded that all she needed was to say, "No!"

A few days later, I went and sat in my favourite place under the willow trees. For years, I had used a short stump as a seat and spent many an hour praying there and enjoying the endless views. With quietness surrounding me, I sat for a long time just soaking in the beautiful view of Mount Quolaque in the distance, framed by the majestic Maluti Mountains. The birds are particularly noisy across the valley, always filling the air with song. With all this before me, I felt like the psalmist David, I could surely say, "The boundary lines have fallen for me in pleasant places" (Psalm 16:6 NIV). Can I give this all up once again and move? Am I sure this is honestly God speaking to me?

In this moment of inner thought, I felt God direct me to read Genesis chapters 17 and 18, where God promises Abraham and Sarah that "by this time next year, Sarah shall have a son" (Genesis 18:10 ESV). Sarah laughed at the idea when she overheard the promise. Their long wait had not made it easy to believe, but we know the story and, true enough, Isaac was born a year later. In those quiet moments under the willow trees, God tenderly ministered to me, explaining that Dihlabeng had been a "child" to me, a "child we have loved". Now he wanted to give us another "child to love in Dubai", namely, Gateway Church, Dubai. Slowly, I settled my heart and embraced God's promise, yet I was reminded of what Heather had said just a few weeks earlier. Armed and confident, I went in pursuit of Heather; it was time to share the news.

Sovereign moment

Later that morning, I took Heather by the hand and we returned to the sacred spot under the willow trees. I moved a second stump closer, and she sat alongside me quietly, waiting to hear what this was all about. She also practised her "No!" I believe. I took her on the journey, starting with the conversation with Terry and all that had happened, not mentioning the "where". I read the Genesis passage to her and shared how God had promised us "another child". Before I could explain, she interjected and said, "I don't think that's possible," leaving me to explain that it was not a physical child but another church just like Dihlabeng Church. Without any further explanation, I said, "I believe God wants us to move to Dubai!"

Quietly and silently, we looked at each other, and I braced myself. Heather's response was most unexpected: "I can do that," she said. The rest of that time was a blur for me, as I was completely overwhelmed by Heather's response. Before we could go any further, Heather jumped up, explaining that she and Adam would be late for their appointment in Bethlehem if she didn't get going right away. With that, and "I can't believe I'm saying this again! What happened to my 'no!'?" we hugged, laughed nervously, and she was off.

Heather told me how her mind spun as she drove Adam the fifty kilometres to Bethlehem, trying to engage with our young son but digest the news she had just received. When they finished their appointment, Heather took Adam for a mandatory toasted sandwich and milkshake at a small restaurant called Polkadot. Once they had placed their orders, Adam spoke up. "I can't believe we're sitting in a coffee shop in a hardware store in the middle of nowhere!" He was referencing Bethlehem, which had once been a beautiful and prosperous market town but had since fallen into decay and neglect. Enquiring further,

Heather asked him, "So where would you rather be, Adam?" Adam replied quizzically, "Dubai?" Heather was astonished, unsure whether he had overheard their conversation or the discussion about an upcoming trip. She went on to ask him why on earth it would be Dubai? He shared that he just thought it was a very cool place to be.

With these remarkable God moments and Heather's approval, I reached out to Terry Virgo to ask if we could have a conversation. I intended to tell him what had transpired since that strange moment in the car and, if he thought it was a good idea, we were willing to move to Dubai and serve the church there, believing God had called us. Sadly, Terry replied to say that he was at a large, demanding conference and would only be available in ten days. Those were the longest ten days of our lives as we waited to share our life-changing news.

Finally, Terry reached out to us and listened attentively to all I shared. He was quite taken aback but said he would speak to his fellow team members who were currently considering the future of the church in Dubai. A few days later, we were excitedly received as the next possible leaders for this special church community in Dubai. There was no turning back now.

Chapter 30

WE TORE OURSELVES AWAY

I fully appreciate why the apostle Paul used the metaphor of a piece of cloth being torn away as a picture of saying goodbye to his friends and partners in the gospel in Ephesus. Just imagining that graphic image is enough to stimulate a deep emotional response. As news of our call to Dubai was shared, the process of bringing everyone up to speed on what God had initiated began, involving people with whom we had journeyed for over thirteen years. It needed to be a thorough transition, but also one that could meet the very tight deadline of November.

Heather and I loved Dihlabeng Church. It had been our focus for many years and now began the task of releasing it to future leadership and releasing it emotionally as well. Most of the church members had come to faith through our move from Cape Town to Clarens, and so they were like children to us. However, the church had a solid "nations-minded" foundation, and so, with many tears, people gladly received the news. Gavin Northcote bravely stepped in as the interim leader until the next leader could be identified and appointed. It was not an easy task for anybody, but he courageously took it on and the enormity of releasing Heather and me. I still remember a message he preached from Acts 13, referencing the time the Antioch Church sent Barnabas and Saul. Gavin called on Dihlabeng Church to show the same courage and "kingdom-mindedness". As a result of his leadership, Dihlabeng Church didn't see itself as sending us away, but rather as adopting and receiving Gateway Church, Dubai, into its family. Such was the ownership of this special rural community in a small village in Southern Africa, that they found the grace to open their hearts to Dubai.

With our boys all fully behind us, we began the most challenging task of all: deciding what we would do with the farm. Acquiring the farm had been such a divine experience that we felt we had no right to sell it unless God specifically called on us to do that. Furthermore, at the time it felt as if the call to Dubai was a short-term assignment and, ultimately, we would return home to our beloved Kromdraai Farm. Graciously, God provided an ideal couple, Peter and Gail Lambshead, to come and live in our home. They had been living with a prophetic vision of moving to a house in the country with a mountain view, and when they saw a photo of our farm, it immediately resonated with them. They gladly accepted the invitation to care for our property and all our pets.

Seven months

The time frame for our move was very short; in fact, only seven months. Bravely, Heather prepared the home and navigated the conflict that came with such a significant change. On one occasion, she went to greet a guest staying in our accommodation, and he pointed to the view and said,

"You know you live in paradise, don't you?" Heather nodded approvingly, but internally she thought, "If only you knew what we're about to do!" However, God was ever so good to us, and we received much encouragement.

It was also a time of considerable change for our immediate family. Cameron, our eldest, had been undergoing a year of training at Dihlabeng Church, a period that had significantly shaped his life. One of his first responsibilities was to drive to the airport to collect two young ladies who were also joining us for the year of training. En-route, Cameron did the inevitable and spilt a cup of coffee down the front of his previously pristinely white t-shirt. He tried all he could to cover it but had to stand in this rather messy state and wait for the two young ladies to appear. As they approached Cameron, one of the young ladies' eyes met his and, as you can imagine, it was love at first sight. For Lerene, even his coffee-stained t-shirt didn't deter her. Both Cameron and Lerene had committed to a year at the church and agreed to no relationships, but it seemed God had other plans. With their future set, they both decided to embrace time apart, and Cameron committed to a further year's training in a church in Sidcup, south of London, in the United Kingdom. That meant, as we would be heading off to the Middle East, he would be leaving for the United Kingdom.

Richard, our middle son, had set his sights on studying IT at one of our prestigious universities. After much consideration, we were thrilled that he decided to join us for a year in Dubai before commencing his studies. Looking back, we are delighted that Richard had the opportunity to journey with us in those early days in Dubai. He often commented on how much he loved the atmosphere of that unusual city, and even returned there for his engagement to Belinda a few years later. He wanted to share his life in Dubai with her, and these were memorable times for us all.

Adam, on the other hand, was going to be finishing his last three years of schooling in Dubai, and he was set and ready, faster than any of us. We realised that we were going to have to embrace a very different family dynamic as we spread across the nations.

Everywhere your feet will tread, I will give to you

Very soon after responding to God's call to Dubai, Heather and I were due to travel to Morocco to join a team, hosted by David Devenish, a key figure in the Newfrontiers leadership team. This task team had a mandate to help our worldwide church movement understand the dynamics of reaching new nations and different cultures. With the growing influence of Newfrontiers across the nations, this was becoming a high priority, and we knew there was much to learn and consider. It was in these meetings that I slowly got to know David Devenish and understand the great wealth of knowledge and experience he carried. This thrilled me, and he started to become a father-like figure to both Heather and me, someone we grew to trust and lean on in our time of transition.

Visiting Morocco was a delightful experience, and we then travelled on for our first visit to Dubai. I had previously visited Dubai a few years earlier, but I had never truly engaged with the city. Now, with Heather, we had the opportunity to meet the incumbent leaders and get a sense of the city. It was July, and it was sweltering. Once before in Egypt, we had experienced severe heat, and this was equally challenging. Nothing can prepare you for temperatures in the high forties. There was a great deal to manage over those few days, and we had many moments when we questioned our plans, which is not uncommon with any significant move. Clive and Heather Curnik served us exceptionally well, and they provided us with the most favourable experience of what was to become our new home.

Only one thing left to do

Over the next five months, I travelled back to Dubai twice, leaving Heather on the farm. Gavin Northcote accompanied me, which was greatly appreciated as it gave me a chance to share my thoughts, both good and bad. On one occasion, after a rather difficult meeting, Gavin asked me how I was feeling. My response was, "I don't want to talk about it!" which we still recall and laugh about. Sheikh Zayed Road is the main highway that takes you through the heart of the city of Dubai. It has six lanes on either side of the freeway, and it is always jam-packed. As one passes through the new part of the city, one can only look on in wonder at the buildings that tower overhead. Their far-reaching creativity is awe-inspiring. Sitting in the back of a taxi on my second visit, I was trying to get my head around this becoming our home. We had lived on the farm for thirteen years, with our nearest neighbour about a mile away. It could not have been more of a contrast to what I was seeing. My heart went out to Heather, who was facing another big move.

Right then and there, I reached out to God. I remember praying, "Lord, you gave us such a love for our farm and all it encompasses, and we have loved it. Now, will you give us the same love for this city? Will you move our hearts for this place?" It was a heartfelt prayer and one that I so needed to be answered if we were going to prosper in Dubai. I'm glad to say that we grew to truly love Dubai, which remains a place we often refer to as "home away from home" to this day. God is faithful.

There was only one thing left to do. It was time to move.

Chapter 31

ON TO THE REGIONS BEYOND

Leaving Clarens, our farm, and our cherished church community coincided with my fiftieth birthday celebration. I was thankful to the friends and family who travelled in for the occasion, which also served as an opportunity to say farewell. It was a memorable time, filled with emotion and the reality of many changes ahead. It was October 2009, and in a few weeks we would be arriving in Dubai, though everything depended on our visas arriving on time. It was also time to say goodbye to Cameron, who was heading off to the United Kingdom, but we were delighted to host Lerene for a few weeks before she left for university in Cape Town.

Dihlabeng Church put on a very special day as they prayed for us, and our ties were further loosened. The emotion of the day was beyond words, but it was ideally captured when the church presented us with two paintings, painted by Gavin and Lynne Northcote's daughter, Sarah. The first was a portrait of Japela Semaase, smiling happily, with such an expression of joy. I was completely undone, seeing the accuracy of his portrait and realised that leading him to Christ sixteen years earlier had led us to this place of sending. Opening the second painting was equally emotionally charged, as it was a portrait of Mme Puleng. She was a dear Basotho grandmother in our community who, like many, made a home for her grandchildren as HIV/AIDS had devastated our community and impacted her family. She had become the "face of the poor" for us, and we had used her photo in various publications relating to our "Embracing the Poor" task team. These two portraits would remain a constant reminder of where we had come from and a reminder to "Remember the Poor" no matter where we were in the world.

Goodbye to Kromdraai

Having obtained our visas, we finally left the farm in early December 2009. Although it is not fully understood, considerable research has been conducted on the notion that farms create a stronger bond with their owners than houses in a city or town. It may be the generational responsibility that lies at its heart, or simply the realisation that someone years before had carved out of the wild landscape the land that became fruitful. Whatever the reason, it was very real for us. The final goodbyes to our faithful and reliable staff, with the promise that they would always be looked after, or the final pats and hugs for our pets, made leaving a very emotional experience. The family packed into our friend's car, and, tearfully, we made our way down the drive towards new adventures. Never did we imagine it would be ten years before we called Kromdraai Farm home again.

Thirteen years earlier, we had left Cape Town with Simon Pettit's prophetic charge, "You do know this will be much bigger than you think." And it had been, much, much bigger.

As we headed to the airport, I was reminded of a similar prophetic insight that was shared with me just a few days earlier. Peter Bonney, who had been a constant support over the years, embraced me and said in his inimitable way, "Stevie, you know this is going to be very big and successful, I have no doubt at all."

With that, it was on to the regions beyond.